BUSHWACKED BY BUSHMASTERS

WACO, THE RAW TRUTH

by
Ronald Davidson

Library of Congress Catalog Card Number 95-94001

ISBN 0-9645223-0-6

Printed in the United States of America

Dedicated to Jim Arrabito, one of the last Americans to leave Baghdad before the fireworks began. A man whose traveled in the narrow lanes and travailed in the wide ones. Jim was living proof that we can do all things through Christ Jesus, who strengthened us.

And to those agents and Davidians dying as a result of the evil ploy they both were victims of.

And of course, to my Collie dog "Charlie", whose fervent desire to rescue someone, kept me going.

PREFACE

As I began to write this book,the one year anniversary of the fire that consumed the 85 people inside the Mt. Carmel Center near Waco, Texas, was only one week away. It seemed much, much further in the past than just one year.

How could it be that time itself has even taken on a different feel, as well as so many other elements of our lives? Like so many other facets that are part of our human makeup, time and how we relate to it, is distinctly different for each of us.

I can recall being told by a local radio talkshow host, upon bringing up the Waco standoff during his show, that he was bored with the subject. He had "had it up to here" with David Koresh and his band of Davidians. This conversation taking place a mere two weeks after the standoff began. And I'm sure this talkshow host was echoing the feelings of many others across the nation. In modern Amerika, I wonder how long it would take for the crucification of Jesus to become a boring subject, were it to have occurred in April of 1993?

We have so many topics to involve ourselves with. Much as Alvin Toffler wrote about our overabundance of consumer choices in the future , in his 1970's book, "Future Shock", we now have an overabundance of choices in the area of human conduct. This book is designed to engage the reader in walking in the writer's footsteps, looking at evidence that has never before been tied together, that attempts to place the events occurring in Waco, within a much larger, much more sinister (if that is possible) government attempt to affect our thinking in ways it deems is in our best interest.

Although time will tell whether our government knows best, I prefer to publish the evidence I have uncovered, and that has, heretofore, been suppressed by the so-called "free press", and let the Amerikan public decide if "Big Bubba knows best".

We will journey through the ATF preparation for, and execution of, the assault on the Mt. Carmel Center. We will examine the events that transpired during the 51 day standoff and subsequent fire that consumed all but nine people inside the Center. I will present the crucial evidence that the Attorneys for both the prosecution and defense produced in court during the subsequent trial of the 12 defendants indicted. I will include an interview with one of the survivors able to withstand the shootout of February 28, 1993, the subsequent standoff and fire, and escape indictment (at least as of this writing).

We will then journey into the unknown world of government motivation for its clandestine activities involving U.S. citizens. This journey will have a definite foreign flavor, involving the World Trade Center bombing, the Atlanta branch of the Banca Nazionale del Lavoro, whose open checkbook was able to bring us the Persian Gulf War (indirectly, of course), smart weapons and all. We will even drag the Pontiff of Rome into this sordid mess, beanie not so upright afterward.

We will read one of the Seven Seals David Koresh decoded and a review of Koresh's handiwork by two Doctors of Divinity from Houston. So, turn off the television, open your mind, and use that brilliant mind your creator endowed you with to reason with my evidence.

THE A.T.F. HEY BUTCH, WHO ARE THOSE GUYS?

When I arose on February 28, 1993, to enter yet another beautiful day in paradise, the letters "ATF" were as far removed from my consciousness as the idea that up on the planet Mars, someone has sculpted a face in the soil. But in the next 51 days that would change, for me and most all citizens that have acquired the daily habit of reading a newspaper.

Suddenly, each day, headlines would stare out at newspaper junkies like myself, telling us new and dramatic tales of a bizarre group of folks, holed up in a large and spacious group of tightly packed structures that became forever known as the "Branch Davidian Compound".

Compound? What is a "compound"? Just the word itself sounds like an injury to the human anatomy with a bone protruding through the skin. I recall a conversation with one of the nine survivors of the Mt. Carmel Center fire, David Thibodeau. In the course of our conversation, as I referred to the Center as the Compound, David continually had to correct me. He kept reminding me that the word "compound" was a government creation, picked up by the media and repeated, continually, by the media.

This may sound like a minor, trivial part of the siege on the Davidians in Waco, but as the noted linguist, the late S.I. Hayakawa once noted, "a subtlety here, a subtlety there is what slanted writing is all about."

We humans think in words. And over time, language begins to form our feelings and emotions. What starts out as minor and trivial, repeated over a period of time, begins to unconsciously shape our thinking.

Over the next forty days I would adjust my satelitte dish each morning to hone in on the daily press conferences being controlled by the FBI and the ATF, and televised from the Waco Convention Center in Waco. And just as men without identities would control who could enter and observe the future trial of the eleven people indicted for alleged crimes committed before, during, and after the Mt. Carmel Center raid, so also was control asserted to pick and choose who could attend and ask questions of these public servants heading our law enforcement agencies at the highest federal level.

It was remarkable to watch at least one hundred reporters fall over each other to keep from hurting the feelings and sensitivities of the parties giving the press conference. Both the ATF and the FBI would, periodically, during the week, change personnel assigned to talk to the press on any particular day. After about two weeks of these progressive weekly, and very often daily, changes in personnel responsible for informing the public about planning for the "dynamic entry" attempted by the ATF, and subsequent Davidian-FBI standoff, I began noticing what appeared to be a pattern.

It seemed that as the press corp got bolder, and more invasive with the quality and specificity of their questions, and started almost cross-examining these government spokesmen, many of the questions answered the previous day would be related back to. If the previous day's questions were related to knowledge the Davidians possessed concerning the timing of the raid, the ATF always came up with a different agent to debrief the press corp.

It wasn't until well into the standoff that David Troy, the Head of Intelligence Operations for the ATF, showed up to take charge of "damage control." By the time Troy arrived, the cat was already out of the bag.

Eventually, Troy would enter the Waco Convention Center (its a Center, not a compound), amble up to the podium, peer down at the assembled group of anxious reporters, and announce to them as if they were Lazarus at the rich man's table waiting for a few factual crumbs that would fall from the table, that the ATF would no longer take questions and give answers. Any questions in the future must be submitted in writing to the ATF, and the ATF would assign the proper laison to answer in due time.

Uh, beg your pardon? Did you just tell the press and the Amerikan public they were mistaken in believing you were a federal agency given authority by Congress to act in the interest of the taxpaying Amerikan public? Did I hear you correctly? Did you just tell the Amerikan public that the agency in whose Department of Intelligence Operations you are in charge, that you had given the green flag to send 104 agents in three cattle cars, into a religious edifice that housed 150 women, children, and adults, to ascertain whether one of their group had violated tax laws and, might be in possession of weapons made illegal six years prior to the date of the assault? Mr. Troy, did you just tell the Amerikan public to kiss your ass?

Who are these guys?

The Bureau of Alcohol, Tobacco, and Firearms (ATF) hasn't occupied its position in the maze of bureaucracies that dot the federal landscape for very long. The ATF came into the maze, formally, in 1972.

Yet, historically, the federal government has legislated rules and regulations relative to the taxation and control of alcohol, tobacco, and firearms that reaches as far back into American history as two-hundred years ago.

As far back as 1791, revenue acts aimed at taxing both alcohol and tobacco, also delegated funds for the offices of tax inspector, collector, and supervisor. During the succeeding century, this cog in the machinery of government went through a variety and frequency of name changes that paralleled the tax rate changes themselves. And of course, motivation to tax never waned during this period. Government bureaucrats have never seen a tax they didn't like.

After the Civil War, "revenuers" battled moonshiners throughout the south in some of the bloodiest opposition federal law enforcemen has ever seen. This writer's father, born on the banks of the Mississippi River in Vicksburg, Mississippi, told stories of revenuers coming down south during prohibition and bribing the backwoods country boys to help them locate illegal stills.

Those boys might have been from the backwoods, but they had learned to get the bribe money upfront, before taking the revenuers up the creek hollows to sniff out the stills because many times the revenuers wouldn't be coming back.

Revenue agents and Deputy U.S. Marshals by the score, were killed as they roamed the hills and hollows searching out the ever elusive illicit stills.

Prohibition changed the government's focus from taxing booze, to an outright ban on it. This made the revenuer's job even more dangerous.

After 12 sordid years, and lots of lost revenue, the government recinded Prohibition via passage of the 21st Amendment in 1933. Tax coffers were as hungry for dollars as the populace was for liquor. Created as a result of the Prohibition Repeal, the Alcohol Tax Unit was established as a tax-collecting branch within the Internal Revenue Service.

But legalizing booze didn't bring to an end the control organized crime had over larger cities within U.S. borders. Well armed and well organized, and politically well connected, organized crime still held sway over the various rackets it had come to dominate.

The Treasury, in what it considered a stroke of genius, decided in 1934, to impose a tax on the gangster's weapons of choice. Rather than attempt an outright ban on sawed-off shotguns and machine guns, a tax would accomplish two goals with one stroke of the legislative pen. It would raise revenue and allow the Feds to keep an eye on any citizens willing to register their weapons. And knowing that no self-respecting mobster would register his Tommygun, much less pay the tax on it, the registration rules would generally only have a practical effect on the non-gangster citizen. Welcome to one of the first intrusions into the Second Amendment, the right of the people to keep and bear arms.

As we are beginning to discover, government intrusions into our U.S. Citizen's Bill of Rights as defined in the U.S. Constitution, always begin with what appears to be the most noble ambitions.

The Clinton Administration, in April of 1994, has chosen to launch a gun search policy to permit police, without warrants, to raid and search public housing apartments, starting in Chicago. President Clinton outlined the policy in his weekly radio address, including in it a tough pitch for his pending anti-crime bill. He contrasted constitutional fears about unlawful searches, with the needs of public housing residents suffering "bloodshed and terror."

The policy grew out of a conflict in August 1993, between the Chicago Housing Authority and the American Civil Liberties Union over an Authority-sponsored, warrantless "sweep" of the Robert Taylor Homes in Chicago, by police searching for guns.

In April 1994, a federal judge reaffirmed a ban on "sweeps", siding with the ACLU in ruling them to be a violation of Fourth Amendment rights prohibiting unlawful search and seizure.

Clinton then ordered Attorney General Reno

and Housing and Urban Development Secretary Henry Cisneros to devise a way to protect public housing residents without trampling the Constitution. The new policy earmarks $28.8 million in new or "reprogrammed" funds for security and crime prevention in Chicago's 135,000 public housing units.

But Cisneros made clear that the new sweeps plan---the core of the policy---was designed not only for Chicago but "so that other housing authorities across the country would be able to act upon it." Well isn't that special. And such noble ambitions.

Because the new 1934 regulations dealt with a tax, rather than a prohibition, it fell to the Treasury Department to enforce the law as part of the Treasury Department's role in collecting all funds due the government. Within Treasury, the Alcohol Tax Unit seemed the logical branch to enforce the new law.

Registering and taxing stills didn't call for the Feds to summon up much more bureaucratic skill than would be necessary for them to register and tax weapons. Sniffing out gun powder, as opposed to mash potatoes, proved comparatively easy for this new branch.

The Alcohol Tax Unit wasn't overwhelmed with registrations of weapons, and by the 1940's time-consuming tax evasion investigations were negligible. As gangsters declined in number and learned how to bend ears in the political arena, so did the use of machineguns and sawed-off shotguns. Enforcement of alcohol taxes once again was the main focus.

In 1951, the Alcohol Tax Unit began enforcing federal taxes on tobacco, thus prompting a name change in 1952 to the Alcohol and Tobacco Tax Division. Once again, the unit considered no new and innovative skills were needed to collect taxes on tobacco anymore than booze and guns. In 1968, jurisdiction over the criminal use of explosives and bombs was extended to the IRS through passage of the Omnibus Crime Control and Safe Streets Act and the Gun Control Act.

This 1968 crime act was very specific in defining specific federal offenses involving firearms. As a result of these new and enlarged powers, the Treasury Department, on July 1, 1972, created the Bureau of Alcohol, Tobacco, and Firearms, under the oversight of the Assistant Secretary of the Treasury for Enforcement, Tariffs and Trade, and Operations.

And subsequent to the formation of the ATF, the 1976 Arms Export Control Act, the 1982 Anti-Arson Act, and the 1978 Contraband Act, have expanded and enhanced the ATF's power and responsibilities over the U.S. citizenry.

Like many government agencies whose parameters expand, tax revenues have also expanded. For example, in 1991, the ATF collected $7.7 billion in alcohol taxes and $4.8 billion in tobacco taxes.

The ATF has developed considerable skill and expertise in arson investigations. In fact, it is the ATF that developed nationwide standards for fire investigations, a subject we will examine in more detail later.

The raid on the Branch Davidians at Mt. Carmel was allegedly for violations of contemporary firearms laws. How the ATF managed to include activities not related to their delegated duties bestowed on them by the Treasury, in the so-called search warrant signed by Magistrate Green, is clearly an ultra-virus wandering outside their authority.

The federal government, from its earliest formation, has actively and openly admitted it has actively suppressed any effort by the disaffected and unhappy citizenry to ban together into armed groups, however small the group, petty the complaint, or grandiose the ambition (Source: Treasury Department Report On The Investigation Of David Koresh). And this discomfort with such citizenry predates the Constitution itself. Freedom of association, another one of the Bill Of Rights, has been particularly difficult for the federal government to extend to its people when the group involved was gaining the ability to wean itself off the fed's hind tit.

Of course, in modern society, in the United States as well as many places throughout the world, humankind is in an uproar. Communities no longer have the social cohesion they had even ten years ago. Deficit spending at a rate never seen in our history, economic recession that has extended into the mid-nineties, staggering increases in inner-city violence as the result of drug wars, and many other factors lend themselves to individuals, sharing like values, voluntarily deciding to create new and different communal living arrangements. American society is ripe for upheavals where rational thinkers, intent on survival for their families and friends, begin to approach social psychology from a new and different angle.

Discomfort over armed organizations banding together to protect their traditional way of life, predates the Constitution. The rebellious outbreak that became known as Shays' Rebellion in 1786, helped spur on the motivation to form a more centralized national government.

During this uprising Massachusetts farmers facing foreclosures on their farms, banded together to keep the courts from issuing executions on the foreclosure judgments. These "regulators", as they called themselves, formed a small army and captured the arsenal at Springfield. They would survive for the better part of five months with this attempt. This action by these farmers was a catalyst for the thirteen states, then in existence, to meet in Philadelphia and design our present form of Constitutional government.

One of the first acts of the newly formed federal government in 1792, was to pass legislation empowering the president to call out the state militias to suppress any insurrection beyond the civil authority's ability to control. Strangely enough, the first occasion to invoke this authority occurred during the federal government's attempt to charge a whiskey tax. The resultant uprising became known as the Whiskey Rebellion of 1794.

Numerous outbreaks of armed opposition to various federal laws, taxes, and perceived oppressive acts would occur over the next one-hundred years.

In 1799 Fries Rebellion against a federal tax on housing, slave rebellion during the 1840's and 50's prompted the government to call out the military and John Brown's ill-fated raid on Harper's Ferry, and his thwarted attempt to rip off its arsenal and distribute it to southern slaves, brought out the Feds to bring it to a halt.

In more recent times, the federal government has shown itself even more impatient with organized, armed groups than it had historically. And the Feds don't appear to distinguish between which end of the political spectrum these groups come from.

In the early 1970's the Symbionese Liberation Army launched its infamous "people's war" by gunning down an Oakland,California, schools superintendent who wanted to create a system requiring students to carry I.D. cards. The SLA also kidnapped newspaper heiress Patricia Hearst, and helped finance their various operations by robbing banks and stores.

The Feds responded by dedicating its resources to tracking down the remaining members, engaging them in a fierce gun-battle and lighting them and the house they were occupying on fire.

Likewise, a man from Arkansas named Gordon Kahl had his own idealogical bone to pick with the federal government. Kahl, a member of the group known as Posse Comitatus, refused to recognize any governmental authority above the county level and acted on his belief by going to prison for refusal to pay federal income tax.

When Kahl remained adamant in his beliefs, even after prison time, the Feds came to Kahl's property to arrest him for alleged violations of his probation. A shootout ensued and Kahl fled his property with two dead agents remaining. Over the next five months Kahl allegedly was housed by persons sympathetic to his plight. The FBI eventually tracked him down, shot him and burned the Smithville, Arkansas, farmhouse in which he was being housed.

In another, somewhat related incident, the FBI pursued a man named Robert Matthews, a member of a group known as The Order. The Order allegedly shared some of the views of Gordon Kahl. Matthews was accused by the FBI of various crimes, including bank robbery and armored car heists, as well as allegedly murdering Denver disk jockey and talkshow host Alan Berg.

Again, after an aggressive pursuit and violent skirmishes in both Idaho and Oregon, Matthews was cornered in northern Washington State and shot. Needless to say, at this point, the structure he was housed in was burned.

Why the fascination with burning? As one of my colleagues working on a documentary about the Waco incident said when I asked him, " No building, no evidence."

As I write, there is an article in the

Los Angeles Times, dated April 18, 1994. Six men were arrested for wearing military type clothes and using the Angeles National Forest for a training ground.

The charges were somewhat vague, one being conspiracy to commit an offense against the United States. Nothing has been forthcoming as to what the crime was. In fact, Rita Mears, the Forest Service's resident special agent for the Angeles National Forest, said she wasn't sure what their agenda was. Yet, these six were still arrested.

Who are these guys? Who are these civil servants hired by our government to protect and serve?

This brief history tells us that, over the centuries, an attitude has developed that may be intensifying. Is this intensity due to a more unpredictable populace, or are we seeing the words of Lord Acton being illustrated in live action, and, in the case of the Branch Davidians, seen live on television, "Power corrupts, and absolute power corrupts, absolutely."

FINDING PROBABLE CAUSE TO SADDLE UP

The ATF claims it had its attention drawn to the Mt. Carmel Center occupants when Sheriff Daniel Weyenberg of the McLennan County Sheriff's Department contacted the Austin, Texas ATF offices, to make ATF aware that "suspicious" deliveries were being received by its residents.

Allegedly, Weyenberg was told by a UPS deliveryman that upon delivering a package to the "Mag Bag", a name given a small auto-repair business employing a few Davidians, and located a few miles from the Mt. Carmel Center, some inert grenades had "inadvertently" fallen out of the package.

According to the Treasury Department Report detailing its investigation of David Koresh, Weyenberg was aware that the Mt. Carmel residents were in the process of constructing what appeared to be a barracks-type structure, had buried a school bus, and were known to have had at least one confrontation with violence attached. Apparently, the good Deputy Sheriff thought, this was sufficient to call in the Feds. Ignored was the fact that Davidians had lived in the area over 60 years.

In the background, as is often the case, were other factors that were driving those in positions of authority to scope in on the residents of the Mt. Carmel Center.

For one, Marc Breault, the so-called self-styled "prophet" (or is that spelled profit?) and one-time second-in-command at Mt. Carmel, had a long bone to pick with David Koresh. As revealed in the "mag rag" Marc wrote with Author Martin King, "Inside The Cult", Marc couldn't keep silent any longer about David Koresh's penchant for bedding under aged lambs in his flock. Breault reveals, to the envy of all contributers to The National Enquirer, Star, and Globe, that he had ragged on the McLennan County Sheriff's Department for years before they would take any action.

Problem is, the Department of Child Protective Services had made two prior, in-depth investigations, and came away convinced there wasn't a shred of evidence to support any claims of either underage sexual misconduct, or inappropriate corporeal punishment of adolescences living at Mt. Carmel.

This leads the rational inquisitor to wonder what other motivations may have been brewing for the Feds to take such an apparently inane group of religious isolationists, such as the Branch Davidians, and place the public's dwindling tax dollars toward giving them their fifteen minutes in the world spotlight.

After all, the FBI had been given the "sikem" by the Justice Department to investigate the Davidians in April of 1992, during the same time Joyce Sparks was investigating Koresh for child abuse allegations. And just as Child Protective Services closed their books without charges, so the FBI in June of 1992, apparently found nothing to substantiate claims made, and closed their investigation.

More will be illuminating our consciousness in future chapters, concerning what may have motivated the Feds to scope in on the Branch Davidians. But on the record, at least, Koresh and his folks passed through the first fire without getting burned.

So Deputy Sheriff Weyenberg piqued the inquiring mind of the ATF and through Special Agent Davy Aguilera, set about gathering enough incriminating evidence of arms violations to attempt convincing a local magistrate there was sufficient probable cause to enter Mt. Carmel and see what all the shouting was about.

Most of the shouting, as Special Agent Aguilera would discover, while engaging in the ever challenging world of fooling former Davidians and gun dealers, by lying about who Aguilera really was, was being done by disgruntled former members and relatives of current members.

In addition to allegations made by Marc Breault, Robin Bunds, one of David Koresh's former lovers and the mother of one of his sons, would also claim the "House of David" got so full of concupiscence, she had to flee.

Needless to say, love hath no fury.....Bunds would cooperate when Aguilera came calling. The parents of two young women inside the Mt. Carmel Center, Isabella Andrade and Jaylene Ojena, would actually enter the Mt. Carmel Center three months prior to the raid to check out the scene and check on Isabella Andrade's daughters. Aguilera would debrief them after their exit.

David Block, another former student of the Davidian theology, and, like Robin Bunds, a California resident, would supply the ATF with its most recent information about the layout of the Mt. Carmel Center.

Block had allegedly been deprogrammed after his experience as a student of the Davidian theology. Generally, a court of law will not allow evidence to be introduced involving subjectmatter over which a party has voluntarily undergone hypnosis. The rationale being that declarant's memory as to the specific event is unreliable post-hypnosis.

Apparently, federal government agents have no difficulty in formulating its largest dynamic entry raid plan based on information supplied them by a party not qualified to take the witness stand, in a court of law, to testify about that same subjectmatter.

According to the Treasury Department Report On The Investigation Of David Koresh, Block would tell the ATF the layout of the Mt. Carmel Center, the routine of the men and women as they engaged in their daily chores, the location of the armory where the weapons were kept, sleeping arrangements of the men and women, what type of weapons were possessed by those inside the Mt. Carmel Center, and with what regularity the inhabitants had weapons on their persons.

One major problem with the ATF's willingness to rely on Block's details, is the fact that Block hadn't been inside the Center since May of 1992. The local law enforcement agencies began conducting SWAT team maneuvers within earshot of the Mt. Carmel Center in

March of 1992. It appears that Koresh interpreted these maneuvers as "sabre rattling" of the most intimidating form. It was subsequent to these maneuvers that Koresh chose to close ranks.

Koresh began to call back members from California and England. He began to make large purchases of weapons parts and acquired chemicals which could be used to make explosives (if one believes the government version of Davidian purchases).

Koresh is also alleged to have purchased night vision scopes and sensors, and large amounts of ammunition. As we will learn in reviewing the trial of the 11 Davidians indicted for murder and conspiracy to commit murder, as well as weapons charges, prosecutor Bill Johnston focuses on this time-frame of March 1992, as the demarcation point in which the level of intensity was raised to a fever pitch.

It is alleged by the ATF, that prior to March 5, 1992, the Mt. Carmel Center possessed approximately 80 firearms. After March 5, the Davidians allegedly obtained an additional 143, claiming most of the additional weapons were "assault rifles" (Source: Treasury Department Report On The Investigation Of David Koresh).

Curiously, the ATF claims they did not find out about the local SWAT team conducting exercises in March of 1992, until after the ATF's failed assault February 28, 1993. If the reader buys that claim, may I suggest immediate withdrawal from present and future reruns of Don Knotts and Andy Griffith's version of law enforcement in Mayberry. Restrictions on viewing old Dragnet and Efrem Zimbalist FBI reruns has shown to regenerate brain cells in laboratory rats. And most Doctors agree listening to Tibetian chants in stereo night after night, has been known to create an irrestible impulse in some Federal agents to commit acts of arson in Texas.

In the beginning of Special Agent Aguilera's focus on Davidian arms of destruction rather than arms of lovemaking, he followed the paper trail left behind by their purchases. Having a Harvard Lawyer residing at Mt. Carmel for legal counsel, didn't seem to impress Agent Aguilera. He may have discovered Law Schools in the U.S. don't include the Second Amendment as part of the curriculum when studying Constitutional Law. Breaching the subject is beneath dignified students of law.

Aguilera had determined that Olympic Arms had shipped a quantity of AR-15 parts to the Mag Bag, and he learned that Henry McMahon, a local gun dealer doing business out of his home as Hewitt Handguns, had sold in excess of a dozen AR-15 lower receivers to Koresh some months earlier.

We discover that Henry McMahon had recently moved to the Waco area from Florida, and started dealing weapons to the Davidians in substantial quantities. Special Agent Aguilera had begun to debrief Lieutenant Gene Barber of the Sheriff's Department, to flush out any additional facts that might facilitate Aguilera's pursuit of the sometimes evasive probable cause necessary to obtain a magistrate's signature on a search warrant.

Barber told Aguilera the Sheriff's Department had referred the same matter previously to the Waco office of the Federal Bureau Of Investigation. And as we previously learned, the FBI didn't pursue the case once they felt comfortable evidence of criminal conduct wasn't sufficient to continue investigating.

But we also learn Bill Johnston, an Assistant U.S. Attorney within the United States Justice Department, the same department in charge of the FBI, was actively encouraging the ATF, through Agent Aguilera, to pursue a case against the Davidians.

Further, we will discover that Johnston took an active role in making contacts available for Aguilera to pursue his goals, was instrumental in raid planning by rendering legal advice to ATF agents (going so far as to tell the planners he wouldn't request a search warrant were the raiders content to seek a "siege" option rather than a "dynamic entry" (Source: The Treasury Department Report On The Investigation Of David Koresh).

Johnston also participated in negotiations during the 51 day stand-off, and to top it off, completed his coup de grace of holistic lawyering, prosecuted the eleven Davidians for, among other charges, murder and conspiracy to commit murder.

Only a jury of twelve ordinary citizens could buck Johnston off the Trojan Horse (the code name given to the operation) Johnston tried to ride through the blood, gore, guts, and veins in his teeth. Until this writer penned the above facts to paper, the public has been convinced it was the ATF that looked like blundering idiots doing a bad imitation of the three stooges dressed in black ATF drag. No, no, no, machinegun breath. Look closer, much closer.

There was lots of talk after the raid and subsequent standoff, about merging the ATF and FBI into one giant "Rambo for Reno" outfit. Any thinking bureaucrat will see the foolishness of such a plan. Separately, the FBI has the best of both worlds; dynamic action without accountability. And if a dynamic entry of the Waco type results in deaths of both agents and civilians, in a fashion unacceptable to the Amerikan public, dismiss a few sacrificial drone clones, display to the citizenry the agency's cleansing procedure, and get set for the next action. So far, its a resounding success.

As Agent Aguilera continued his paper chase of the Davidians proclivity toward the machinegun way of life, he concluded neither Koresh, nor any of his flock, were licensed federal arms dealers or manufacturers. Further, no Davidians had registered any National Firearms Act weapons.

The National Firearms Act, codified in Chapter 53 of Title 26, United States Code, sets out comprehensive tax and registration systems governing the manufacture, transfer and possession of certain firearms. Among firearms covered by the Act are machineguns (26 U.S.C. 5845(b).

In addition, 18 U.S.C. 922(0) makes it unlawful for any person to transfer or possess a machinegun unless the machinegun was lawfully registered before May 19, 1986, the effective date of the Firearms Owners Protection Act of 1986 (why the Act's title includes "Protection" only a bureaucrat well-versed in Orwellian newspeak can answer that).

Before this Act, it was legal for citizens to make, sell, and possess machineguns so long as they complied with the taxing and registration requirements of the National Firearms Act. Since 1986, no machineguns have been permitted to be manufactured in the United States, except those used by government agencies or for export.

This tells us that if the Davidians had engaged in the same alleged conduct in December of 1985, that they were accused of in 1992, approximately six years earlier, they would have been doing <u>NOTHING</u> illegal. Did Agent Aguilera investigate to see if the Davidians involved in arms purchases, had knowledge of their possible violations before pursuing his investigation? Or did the ATF's true goals make intent irrelevant?

Assuming the Davidians had knowledge of their offenses, was the ATF justified in sending two cattle cars with approximately 106 agents intc the Davidian dwelling housing over 150 men, women, and children, to gain conformity to a law enacted just six years prior?

Although Agent Aguilera concluded that none of the Davidians were licensed federal arms dealers, on what basis did he conclude this? None of his contacts were with current members of the Mt. Carmel Center, at least none on record. And when the ATF was required to produce its raid plan (the plan produced would later prove to be concocted, for the most part, after the raid), the agency revealed it was under the assumption only 75 people lived in the Center. Since the ATF had set up an undercover house within view of the Mt. Carmel Center, with eight agents engaged in around-the-clock surveillance beginning January 11, 1994, why were their estimates so inaccurate?

How could Aguilera conclude none of the Davidians possessed a license to deal in the type of arms they were allegedly possessing? After all, obtaining a license was relatively easy. When Treasury Secretary Bentsen came out in support of additional legislation restricting the issuance of licenses, he stated there were more licensed gun dealers than gas stations in America.

As writer Larry McMurtry later asked, "What were the Davidians doing to provoke the raid? Probably, they were converting semi-automatic rifles to full auto. That certainly is a crime; even possessing the capability to convert them is a crime (McMurtry incorrectly interprets the law on this issue). But down here in the Fifty-Caliber Belt this particular crime is usually treated about as seriously as spitting on the sidewalk (Larry McMurtry, "Return To Waco," The New Republic, June 7, 1993).

This writer can recall stopping at a gas station in Austin, Texas, on my trip back from visiting the burned-out Mt. Carmel Center.

I purchased a key chain made out of a 30 caliber bullet. As I pulled out to get on the freeway, a Texas Department of Transportation sign pointed me toward San Antonio, and under it the words "Don't Mess With Texas" glared back at me. Form over substance.

During my four years of studying law I became aware that most of our common-law that evolved into today's modern statutory law, evolved from English common-law. The two states evolving much of their modern law from Roman common-law, hence, are exceptions to the historical English common-law heritage, are Louisiana and, lo and behold, Texas.

Texas has become, in many ways, an island unto itself. Its populace is a reflection of this in suble ways, one being Texas' romance with weaponry.

For every man, woman, and child in Texas, there is an average of four weapons. Texas people located in more rural, remote areas have different needs with regard to weaponry than other states. The wide open areas in much of Texas requires individuals to take responsibility for their own protection, since a call to 911 may go unanswered or take hours for a response.

In this vein another writer asked: "Who, exactly, were the Davidians bothering? The ATF says they were hoarding guns. How un-American and how un-Texan. May we expect the administration to lay siege now to the National Rifle Association? The Davidians were also said to be abusing children. A graver charge, but not a charge that warrants the ATF's or the FBI's actions (Leon Wiesel,

"The True Fire," The New Republic, May 17, 1993).

A few weeks before the fire that consumed the Mt. Carmel Center, a Washington D.C. columnist raised similiar concerns: "No government official has yet explained what crime was being committed by the dimwits of something called the Branch Davidians....What provoked this show of force from the crack troops of the Bureau of Alcohol, Tobacco, and Firearms? Was someone caught smoking in a restricted area? Were the faithful of the Rev. David Koresh distilling ardent spirits in an illegal still for one of his holy rites? Was there an illicit drug on the premises, or did someone have a shotgun that ran afoul of government standards?....If Americans cannot live the life of the rugged---albeit somewhat loony---individualist in the vast reaches of the great West, where can they live normal American lives? (R. Emmett Tyrell,Jr. "Crystals In The Waco Crucible," The Washington Times, April 4, 1993)

Nonetheless, Agent Aguilera continued to pursue his paper chase. Apparently, he could have stopped the chase as of November 20, 1992, because by then, the party he was trying to please, Bill Johnston, was already satisfied that Agent Aguilera's handiwork was sufficient to convince the local magistrate probable cause existed.

Probable cause, another legal term that has been used, abused, and confused, especially during the recent past in jurisprudence. During just the nineteen-eighties alone, the Supreme Court has changed its definition on three separate occasions.

Although there is no precise, mathematical definition for what constitutes probable cause, the standard to be met by arrest and search warrant applications, the Supreme Court has explained that probable cause to obtain an arrest warrant exists when law enforcement authorities have knowledge of facts and circumstances sufficient in themselves to warrant a belief, by a person of reasonable caution, that an offense has been, or is being committed by the person to be arrested (Beck v. Ohio, 379 U.S. 89,91(1964)).

Probable cause to search exists where there is "a fair probability that contraband or evidence of a crime will be found in a particular place" (Illinois v. Gates, 462 U.S. 213,238(1983)).

Probable cause can be based on any reliable evidence, including circumstantial evidence, hearsay from reliable sources, and information from ANONYMOUS informants as long as its corroborated by other independent evidence (Rule 41(c) of the Federal Rules of Criminal Procedure).

Whether Agent Aguilera had accumulated sufficient evidence to satisfy the above defining of probable cause, is like asking which denomination in the realm of Christianity speaks the real truth? It depends on who you are speaking to.

Bill Johnston was speaking to a magistrate sharing Johnston's view of the evidence. Magistrate Dennis Green issued a search warrant for Mt. Carmel Center, said warrant to be served no later than March 1, 1993.

According to a documentary film titled "Waco, The Big Lie", produced by Linda Thompson, during the time Agent Aguilera was checking out Henry McMahon, one of the gun dealers that had sold David Koresh a substantial number of weapons, and operating his business under the name Hewitt Arms, McMahon is quoted in the Mobile Press column written by Pete Zarrielos saying he called the Mt. Carmel Center while the ATF WAS PRESENT and told David Koresh the ATF was concerned about the number of weapons Koresh was purchasing. McMahon said Koresh told him to tell the ATF to come on out to Mt. Carmel and see for themselves. Needless to say, ATF declined.

As to the claims that none of David Koresh's followers was a licensed gun dealer, in the Treasury Department Report On The Investigation Of David Koresh, Henry McMahon is quoted calling Koresh "my preacher". Isn't this a sufficient nexus to consider whether those Branch Davidians involved in weapons purchases may have been conducting legitimate business? The Treasury Department Report didn't attempt to explain this contradiction.

Upon reading the Treasury Department's version of the tragedy, many parts were laughable when placed under the scope of one trained in legal reasoning. In the Report's discussion of a group of citizens calling themselves Covenant of the Sword and the Arm of the Lord (CSA), the ATF led the assault on the CSA compound April 20, 1985. CSA members retreated farther into their compound, barricading themselves behind their defenses.

The agents set up a siege perimeter and settled in to wait. CSA allegedly used the wait to destroy many of the weapons (hence, evidence).

Negotiators from the FBI arrived and began the tedious, frustrating process of talking the group out. Three days later, on April 22, 1985, James D. Ellison and the 75 members of the CSA surrendered (James Coates, Armed and Dangerous: The Rise of the Survivalist Right, (New York: Hill and Wang, 1987).

Sounds strikingly familiar to the event that occurred at Mt. Carmel. Only the Davidians standoff lasted 51 days. Yet during that entire time the Davidians were unable to dismantle <u>ANY</u> of the alleged 44 automatic rifles they possessed. Their impotence to cover the illegal trail they had allegedly blazed included their apparent unconcern for removing a part the ATF claims was found in the ruble on a metal lathe supposedly used to make machinegun parts.

All those criminal minds, occupying the same living area for 51 days, and it never occurred to any of them to destroy any evidence!!

FINDING THE PROPER SADDLE

FOR THIS TROJAN HORSE

In November of 1992, Bill Johnston reviewed the evidence Aguilera had accumulated that suggested the Branch Davidians may have violated Federal firearms statutes. Johnston was convinced at that time, that the threshold requirements for probable cause had been met.

Normally, once a prosecutor is satisfied that necessary elements for probable cause have been attained, the desire is to move quickly. A magistrate issuing a warrant based on stale evidence (usually within 30 days of obtaining said evidence), may yield to a suppression motion that is inevitably filed by defense attorneys, desiring to keep out of the proceeding any evidence obtained via a stale find. This rule of law is necessary to rein in prosecutors tempted to circumvent criminal procedure rules when dealing with sophisticated suspects.

But as we will continue to discover, the Branch Davidians were getting unique treatment. At a meeting of all the top brass mucky-mucks, including Associate Director Hartnett, Dan Conroy, David Troy, and others on Christmas Eve 1992, they wanted the Special Response Teams plotting an entry strategy to <u>slow down</u> its planning of the raid.

Their reasons for wanting to slow down the operation will be looked at in a later chapter. Concern about stale evidence was non-existent. Concern about destruction of evidence was given equal footing. Hey Judge Smith, suppress this!!!

Aguilera reported to Assistant Special Agent-In-Charge (ASAC) Chuck Sarabyn (Houston), what U.S. Attorney Bill Johnston had told him. A warrant could be procured any time.

Sarabyn assumed responsibility for the tactical planning necessary for executing an entry into Mt. Carmel. Whatever enforcement action chosen, Sarabyn decided, would require at least one Special Response Team (SRT).

SRT's are specially trained groups of ATF agents with special expertise in executing intricate, more involved tactical missions where high-risk warrants are to be served.

Sarabyn arranged a meeting for December 4, 1992 (although for some strange reason he, as principal planner, couldn't be present), to include Sarabyn's superior, Phil Chojnacki, Special Agent-In-Charge (SAC) of ATF's Houston Division, Ted Royster, SAC of the Dallas Division; William Buford, Resident Agent-In-Charge (RAC) of the Little Rock ATF office, a co-team leader of the New Orleans SRT, and an Army Special Forces combat veteran; and James Cavanaugh, ASAC of the Dallas ATF office.

Jerry Petrilli, RAC of the Albuquerque ATF office, team leader of the Dallas SRT, and a Marine Corps combat veteran, would also attend this December 1992 meeting. Two other ATF agents, Kenny King, who would be seriously wounded in the raid, and Curtis Williams, couldn't attend.

Each of these planners had extensive training with the ATF, each having engaged in numerous high-risk raids in search of illegal weapons. In particular, the SRT leaders had extensive law enforcement and military experience.

However, only William Buford, one of the founders of the ATF SRT, had ever engaged in a tactical operation of the magnitude of that contemplated for those folks residing at the Mt. Carmel Center.

Buford was the planner that devised the perimeter control for The Covenant, The Sword, And The Arm Of The Lord action alluded to earlier. According to various sources, Buford would recall, and zealously advocate for this type of siege approach that proved such a success with the CSA folks. Buford was adamant in his opposition to the "dynamic entry" plan that Bill Johnston required and resulted in so many deaths, both of agents and Davidians.

Recall U.S. Attorney Bill Johnston informed the ATF early in the investigation that he wouldn't authorize a search warrant for the Branch Davidian residence if it was to be executed through a siege-style operation. Johnston claimed that such a strategy would permit Koresh and his followers to destroy evidence and make prosecution more difficult.

Had Johnston known what a rousing success playing recordings of Tibetian chants and rabbits being slaughtered over loud-speakers at night would have on the Davidians' desire to destroy evidence, he may have taken a closer look at the "siege" approach. Maybe next time.

Given the layout of the Mt. Carmel Center, situated on very flat terrain, with both a very high tower and a three-story room that enabled its occupants to see for miles, to demand planners focus on only one option not only requires planners to subjugate their areas of expertise to a man untrained in tactics of the kind here employed, it illustrates how the integrity of an agency can be compromised in ways that the untrained eye would overlook. Inquiring minds are motivated to look for other possible explanations for what has proven to be the most disasterous raid in U.S. civilian law enforcement history.

Certainly, the threat of Davidians destroying evidence was a real possibility, were a siege tactic chosen. But when weighing priorities, human lives far outweigh evidence destruction. The maximum penalty for the charges alleged, that the Davidians may have been guilty of possessing illegal weapons, was ten years. Such a violation of federal law pales in comparison to the threat to men, women, and children housed at the Mt. Carmel Center, should a dynamic entry go awry, not to mention potential injury to the agents executing the raid.

Agent Aguilera made it clear to the planners at the December 4, 1992, meeting precisely what they would be up against. He estimated 75 people lived at the Center (an estimate that proved to be far too low). This estimate included large numbers of women and children, all of whom were fiercely loyal to Koresh and dedicated to his religious teachings. Aguilera also laid out the physical aspects of the Mt. Carmel location.

It was at this meeting that the decision

was made to set up a surveillance team to gather more current information on the routines and living arrangements of those inside the Center. And to solicit more facts concerning the interior design of the Center.

Upon conclusion of this December 4, 1992, meeting the leaders of the SRT's, those who specialized in dynamic entry tactics, would be the driving force directing the operation.

In late December the tactical planners met again to review additional information Aguilera had obtained, including reports of interviews with former Davidians, recent photos of the Center, etc. During this period SRT leaders Buford, Williams, Petrilli, and King, were driven to the Center with Sarabyn to see, first hand, what they were up against.

They were struck by how flat the terrain was and how immune the Center appeared to be from either a dynamic entry or a siege. Looking back, the FBI had relatively minor trouble maintaining a perimeter, once the 51 day stand-off began.

In early January, the next convening of the tactical planners occurred. Sarabyn decided to submit a formal request to the Regional Logistics Support Office. This is the office through which the Department of Defense provides non-operational military support.

After submitting this request, Sarabyn sent a superseding request in mid-February. As a result of these requests the military made several flights over the Center and the Mag Bag producing aerial reconnaissance photographs, interpretation of the photos, and use of the Thermal Imaging System during flights to identify "hot spots" at the Center.

These flights were allegedly directed toward the search for armed guards and drug manufacturing facilities. Government experts would later opine that sufficient analysis to ascertain whether drug labs existed at the Center wasn't possible based on the images obtained on these overflights.

Paul Fatta, a Branch Davidian not in attendance when the raid occurred, and allegedly unable to be located by the FBI shortly after the raid, was, nonetheless, able to find good ole Ed Bradley of 60 Minutes fame.

Ed Asked Paul if he could explain the two hot spots showing up on the thermal imaging photos. "Simple," Fatta said. Fatta said it got cold in that part of Texas in February, and when it did those inside the Center would light the two diesel heaters to keep the residents warm. The ATF was beginning to emulate and promote the Mr. Magoo School of Law Enforcement. Can you see how the Magooite approach interfaces with the Barney Fife "Single Bullet Theory" of handgun control for police officers?

In addition to the overflights, the military provided the ATF with the Military Operation Urban Terrain training facility at Fort Hood for training purposes and helped ATF with the setting up of a facility resembling the Mt. Carmel Center.

There has been increasing concern that the military went much, much farther in its assistance to the ATF in their preparations. Soldier of Fortune magazine, in its May 1994 issue, goes so far as to state that four Green Berets donned civvies and watched, first hand, while the actual February 28 raid took place.

James L. Pate, writer for Soldier of Fortune, says his investigation reveals convincingly, that this was far from a rogue operation these Green Berets chose to occupy their time blowing off concussion grenades.

Pate says these men were part of a sanctioned, ongoing program to more involve the military in civilian law enforcement. In 1989, Congress approved a defense authorization bill directing the Pentagon to train and assist "to the maximum extent possible" civilian police engaged in drug interdiction.

The law was partly a response to Defense Secretary Dick Cheney's earlier designation of drug trafficking as a national security threat. After the bill passed, Cheney announced the activation of the Joint Task Force Six (JTF-6) at Fort Bliss, Texas. In 1990 in what became known as the Operation Green Sweep, northern California residents were confronted at gunpoint by men dressed in military garb as helicopters rained down on residents of the King's Range. Truly, these men came ready to battle.

They came not as young American men serving their country. Fresh out of high school, raised in a rural area and just following the Captain's orders. No. These men brought more pain than that. Their mission designed to unnerve, to micro-wave our minds. These men came as aliens from another planet, on a power trip. Replicants out of "Bladerunner." Coming to do the spiritual will of J. Edgar Hoover. Yuk!!!

The Green Sweep military operation would precede a civil lawsuit filed by a local attorney, Ron Sinoway, on behalf of some of the residents scared out of their micro-waved minds by these Replicants pretending to be Amerikans.

After attending the hearing for Summary Judgment in San Francisco Federal Court in September of 1994, I predicted the judge would rule in favor of the Government. Federal courts have no jurisdiction over Replicants.

Nevertheless, during the discovery proceedings Sinoway would give a nightly blow by blow report of how the military was using sophisticated satellite photography capable of detecting whether so much as even a shovel full of dirt has been disturbed from the surface of the Earth.

Myself and my neighbors of Southern Humboldt County would sit each evening transfixed by revelations from the Deputy Replicant Sinoway had under oath and deposed that day. The information KMUD broadcast during the brief period Sinoway had these government officials under oath, was far and away the most sensitive and insightful as to how advanced our electronics are.

This operation was nicknamed "Green Sweep" to buttress government claims they were concerned with stopping marijuana cultivation on the north coast. Magicians success hinges on their ability to control the audience's focus. A more likely motive for "Green Sweep" was to gauge how united people of differing political persuasions would become, when a vital interest common to both sides is threatened. Here, the vital interest is local law enforcement sovereignty, found in the currently defunct Tenth Amendment of The Bill Of Rights.

And what could the Feds reasonably conclude in the aftermath of Green Sweep? Even right-wingers will allow temporary suspension of The Bill of Rights if convinced the end result justifies it. Additional conclusions, the left-wing environmental activists don't speak softly and carry a big stick. They speak loudly and carry a big hooter.

The spell they're under has them believing gun control will increase their power as U.S. Citizens. Does smoking too much dope cause brain damage? I rest my case.

And the lawyer bringing suit against the Federal and State governments in the Green Sweep case. Ron Sinoway is a graduate of Georgetown University Law School. The preferred edifice of future Washington D.C. government clones adherent to the much maligned but inevitable spiritual awakening known as the "Zen-Yuppie" movement.

The spiritually advanced adherents are allowed to occupy rewarding positions such as News Director of various mass-media outlets, or, as is the case in my locale, Rock Music Impresario, non-visionaries need not apply.

In southern Humboldt County, the movement

is convinced their stubborn deity is a closet rastafarian, willing to commune with his subjects after a minimum twenty-four hour marathon of reggae music, hooters mixed with psychedelics of choice (preferably Ecstasy), women dressed in formal Gypsy attire admitted free. Self-mutilation optional, nose-rings only for those holding positions of Rasta-deacon and Rasta-bishop.

Didn't I see these folks at the bottom of Mt. Sinai when Charleton Heston came packin down the mountain side with the two tables of stone? Wouldn't any God fearing, family values supporting, Newt Gingrich cloned republican support suspending The Bill Of Rights of people of this ilk long enough to green sweep their shit off the planet earth?

The writer's too paranoid you say. Too many conspiracy theories in the pot will spoil the stew!!

Shortly after Attorney Sinoway deposed the cremede la creme of drug enforcement agencies, he mysteriously suffered a stroke. And two months before oral arguments were scheduled in the government's motion for Summary Judgment, Sinoway's law office was burned to the ground. Mercifully, Sinoway was spared the Vince Foster treatment.

Foster's death tends to make one wary of coroner claims when suicide is listed as cause of death. The Washington rumor mill ran rampant in March of 1994, with tales claiming Bill Clinton's counsel and keeper of Clinton's Whitewater records, Vince Foster, had actually died in Virginia, his body then transported to Washington D.C. Conspiracy theorists suggesting Park Police investigators could be more effectively controlled than law enforcement in Ollie North's home state.

How deeply involved is the military in civilian law enforcement? The Joint Task Force Six operational manual, Operational Support Planning Guide states: "JTF-6 is intended to serve as force multiplier to law enforcement agencies. It has the potential to enhance law enforcement effectiveness or release significant resources to focus on drug interdiction/seizure actions....using a total force approach."

The planning guide goes on to state: "military forces are precluded by the Posse Comitatus Act from performing search and seizure, arrest, or other similiar law enforcement activities." As the Amerikan public has experienced repeatedly since the 30's Depression, government administrative agencies, like the Hoover vacuum cleaner salesman that comes to your door just wanting to clean your carpet, always want to give us more than we bargained for.

Under the "Political Sensitivities" section, the guidebook suggests employment of military force in such a way that potential confrontation with civilians is avoided (we're now seen as "civilians", not citizens). And the kicker: "Many operations are inherently sensitive and involve various risks which may be heightened by the release of information to the public."

The guidebook further states, "Innovative approaches to providing new and more effective support to law enforcement agencies are constantly sought, and legal and policy barriers to the application of military capabilities are gradually being eliminated. Pending legislative actions may soon alleviate some of these restrictions." Well isn't that special.

Revoking the Posse Comitatus Act with one fell swope of the legislative pen would startle the Amerikan public and awaken them out of their restful sleep. JTF-6 is just the right sedative to get us that few extra winks Sominex simply can't deliver.

During the Branch Davidian trial, Mike DeGeurin, a Houston attorney defending one of the Davidians, asked a government witness if he recognized any of five names that DeGeurin implied were present during the February 28 raid. The five later would be confirmed to be members of the 3rd Battalion, 3rd Special Forces Group, headquartered in Ft. Bragg, North Carolina. In this group of five, one was a major.

These five plus five other Green Berets were among a company of Green Berets deployed in January 1993, from Ft. Bragg to McGregor Range, New Mexico, a remote part of Fort Bliss. These troops were assigned a 90-day stint with the Rapid Support Unit which responds on short notice to requirements generated by JTF-6.

Once the ATF requested military assistance, JTF-6 issued a mission order to this Rapid Support Unit. Mission JT002E resulted in an operational detachment from the 3rd Battalion of the Special Forces Group, deploying to Fort Hood, Texas to train the ATF.

On February 16, 1993, three of the ten

Green Berets mentioned above, Sargeants Chris Dunn , Greg Handy, and Cordell Ackley left Fort Bliss, for Fort Hood, Texas, to survey training sites. The following day they secured the use of Hargrove Military Operations Urban Terrain Training Center. They also met with ATF Agents Kenny King and William Buford, leaders of the Special Response Units mentioned earlier. These two would, come raid time, be injured by gun fire as they sought to make forced entry into the second floor of Mt. Carmel.

Testimony at the trial would indicate their injuries may have been sustained as a result of weapons fire from Agent Keith Constantino. Three members of their Special Response Team, Conway C. LeBleu, Robert Williams, and Todd McKeehan, were killed. Whatever secrets were whispered to these ATF agents by the Special Forces, don't appear to have been effective.

Linda Thompson, an attorney from Indiana, alleges in her film, "Waco, The Big Lie," that three of the four men who died during the assault on the Mt. Carmel Center, were President Bill Clinton's bodyguards during his campaign for the presidency. Whether this is merely coincidence, or there is some hidden meaning, at this juncture I'm clueless. Maybe Vince Foster is resting in peace with the answer.

By February 24, 1993, all ATF personnel had arrived at the Hargrove training site. The Major mentioned earlier in court by attorney DeGuerin, Major Mark Petree, flew to Killeen, Texas on a commercial flight (the military must have been short on planes that day) and was met by two members of the detachment.

Communications training began on February 25, 1993, and again, whatever these "special" forces knew that ATF didn't, certainly wasn't evident on raid day. Communication was deemed to be the weakest link in the ATF's chain that day.

Sheriff Lynch, the party receiving the 911 call made by the Davidians that day, couldn't connect with even the ATF van maintaining the communication equipment, and eventually dispatched one of his own deputies to the scene to assist in orchestrating a cease-fire.

A training schedule was developed February 26, 1993, including live firing. It was necessary to get permission from the Fort Hood Range Control to train the ATF in the use of flash-bang grenades, out of concern for safety.

As was revealed in House Appropriations Committee hearings and in the Treasury Department Report, never was a knock-and-announce entry rehearsed, nor a peaceful entry.

On February 28, 1993, a mere two days of training under their belts, the ATF left Fort Hood to proceed to their staging area near Waco. The caravan of vehicles, with headlights glaring, stretched for over a mile, as this "secret"unit cruised down the open freeway headed for its "undercover" mission.

At least they stopped short of employing megaphones to let the public know what they were up to. The convoy had a cattle trailer at each end, to keep things looking uniform(?), and many vehicles had that unmistakable look only government vehicles possess, four door, late model, Amerikan-made, super-antennas growing out of each rig's roof.

In the Justice Department manual published after the Waco fiasco titled, "Recommendations of Experts For Improvements In Federal Law Enforcement After Waco," it was suggested future excursions such as occurred from Fort Hood to Waco be done via two buses that could more easily mask clandestine raids such as this.

Maybe consideration of a location for the staging area not located next to a busy freeway would be helpful to this end also. After learning of the tactics used by ATF in attempting to keep the raid on the Mt. Carmel Center from coming to the attention of the Davidians, it would have been more of a miracle if those inside had never found out about the planned raid.

In looking back on the raid preparations, it must be remembered that the JTF-6 multiagency rent-a-troop, was designed to provide military resources to civilian law enforcement in the war on drugs. The question of drugs in the ATF's Waco investigation came up at its initial stages. During the daily press conferences given at the Waco Convention Center by the ATF and the FBI, the various reporters asked on at least four separate occasions, whether there were suspicions of illegal drug activity. The answer was always no.

Later, during the 51 day standoff, when reporters' questions gradually became more sophisticated, and to the point, David Troy, Head of Intelligence Division of the ATF, was asked how the ATF was able to obtain permission to use National Guard helicopters. Troy claimed overflights showed a hotspot consistant with a methamphetamine lab. Never mind that such a hotspot would be consistant with numerous other activities, such as, for instance, a diesel heater on a cold February night.

At the trial of the eleven Davidians, not one shred of evidence was produced or even alluded to, that mentioned drug use among the Davidians. Further, toxicology tests performed on the 81 Davidians that died in the April 19, 1993, fire, revealed not one body with so much as even a trace of any illegal substance.

ATF AND THE MEDIA---STRANGE BEDFELLOWS

Modern law enforcement and modern-day mass media share a much more unique position than in times pre-dating video cameras. One never knows when a person with video camera at the ready, may be lurking in the background undetected, or, in the case of Rodney King's videoed live thrashing, from a distant apartment.

Law enforcement has even come to view live videotaping of law enforcement at work, as a potential boon for sorely needed improvements in public relations.

Although the civil trial resulting from the beating Rodney King suffered resulted in a judgment of $3.8 million being assessed against L.A. County, its rare that uncut footage of the type seen in the King beating makes it to national media outlets.

Its one thing to allow the media to ride along filming law enforcement applying their trade on such weekly shows as "Cops" and "Amerika's Most Wanted". Its quite another to allow them to accompany a federal agency, such as the ATF, on the largest dynamic entry raid in law enforcement history.

The day after the assault on the Mt. Carmel Center, ATF spokesperson Sharon Wheeler claimed the media wasn't contacted prior to the raid. This, one of the many, many, bold-faced lies the public was told in the initial stages of the uncovering of the affair, would continue into the very presence of Congressmen in the Appropriations Committee, who began to hold hearings on the affair while the standoff was still in progress.

The media's interest in investigating the Branch Davidians and David Koresh, began in the spring of 1992, strangely enough, about the time that local SWAT team conducted their exercises within earshot of the Mt. Carmel Center.

Reporter Mark England, working for the Waco Tribune-Herald, a newspaper owned by Cox Enterprises headquartered in Atlanta (this connection will be scrutinized in more detail later), was assigned to work up a story biographing the Davidians.

In October of 1992, four months before the raid, Darlene McCormick, a reporter assigned to work with Mark England on the story, called U.S. Attorney Bill Johnston to inquire as to what constitutes an illegal weapon. Good ole Bill told her that "Treasury guys" could tell her if any Branch Davidians had permits for automatic weapons (Source: Treasury Department Report On Waco).

While Johnston claims not to have given McCormick any specific information about the ATF investigation, she rightly concluded that the ATF was investigating the Davidians. Johnston then notified the ATF of the Waco Tribune-Herald story in the works.

Why is it that Bill Johnston keeps blurring the picture? Was he just a legal dork that should never have been allowed out of the law library? Or was he helping facilitate a much larger plan?

By Januray 1993, England and McCormick

had drafted the now infamous "Sinful Messiah" series of articles. One of the primary sources supplying the authors with juicy tidbits detailing the Davidians' lifestyle, and Koresh alleged sexual appetites in particular, was Marc Breault, Koresh's former second-in-command.

Because the "Sinful Messiah" series contained startling revelations of Branch Davidian lifestyles and disclosure of dangerous weapons the Davidians possessed inside the Center, and probably, since much of the information was supplied by Breault and contained a lot of Breault "bullshit", fears of Davidian retaliation became a concern of Randall Preddy, the Tribune-Herald publisher.

Preddy contacted Cox's Vice-President for Security, Charles Rochner. Rochner and Preddy discussed the situation at a publisher's meeting in Orlando, Florida, in February of 1993. Rochner planned to come to Waco later that month.

In mid-January the Tribune-Herald's managing editor, Barbara Elmore, contacted good ole Bill Johnston, manifesting more concern over possible retribution related to the "Sinful Messiah" series.

Johnston arranged a meeting between Elmore, Earl Dunagan, acting Resident-Agent-In-Charge of the Austin ATF office (Dunagan is acting RAC because the former RAC, Larry Sparks, was administratively removed August 5, 1992, and later fired by ATF), and Dunagan's supervisor, Chuck Sarabyn (the Chuckster has been fired as of October 1994).

This meeting was held at the U.S. Attorney's

office in Waco. Johnston admits introducing the parties, but claims he didn't participate in the meeting (Source: The Treasury Department Report on Waco).

Sarabyn made Elmore aware of ATF's ongoing investigation, and asked her to delay publication of the "Sinful Messiah" series. The agents promised to give Tribune-Herald reporters "front-row seats" during the execution of the contemplated law enforcement action if the newspaper delayed publication of its series until after the raid (Source: The Treasury Department Report, page 69). Elmore said she must acquiesce to the desires of her publisher.

And the kicker: Dunagan told Elmore ATF planned to execute the search warrant on February 22, 1993, and he would inform her if the date changed!!

Subsequent to this meeting, the main man in charge of the ATF Waco operation, Phil Chojnacki (fired by ATF in October 1994), assumed sole responsibility for communications with the Tribune-Herald. On February 9, 1993, Rochner (remember, he's out of Atlanta) informed Chojnacki that Rochner would act as the Tribune-Herald's laison with ATF.

Rochner planned to be in Waco the week of February 22, 1993, and Chojnacki agreed to meet with him. And the kicker: Chojnacki invited Rochner to observe raid training at Fort Hood, Texas on February 25, later changing the invitation to the 26th or 27th.

Approximately two weeks subsequent to the meeting Bill Johnston had set up between Dunagan, Sarabyn, and Elmore, Dunagan kept his promise to Assistant Editor Elmore of informing her if the date of the raid changed. With the approval of Chuck Sarabyn, Dunagan told Elmore the raid had been moved to March 1, 1993. Elmore, in turn, notified other Tribune-Herald personnel of the change.

Any reasonable mind looking at these events transpiring between the ATF and the Tribune-Herald, would conclude a high level of cooperation was taking place between the parties. One would assume that, come raid day, the Tribune-Herald personnel would be on the scene. After all, this would be the most massive civilian law enforcement action in modern U.S. history.

Further, ATF media policy requires ATF approval at Washington D.C. headquarters, if media ride-alongs are contemplated (ATF Order 1200,2B, January 20, 1988). However, ATF Assistant Director of Congressional and Media Affairs, James Pasco, claims he was never notified of any contacts with the Tribune-Herald contemplating giving them "front row seats".

Jack Killorin, Chief of ATF's Public Affairs Branch, told Phil Chojnacki bringing the press along on the raid could create an inflammatory situation.

Nevertheless, the damage had already been done. The Tribune-Herald, whether through Bill Johnston and/or ATF design or stupidity, was now a partner.

And the Tribune-Herald quickly became partners with various other media sources. Tribune reporter Tommy Witherspoon, assigned to cover the Waco courtrooms, had a confidential informant keeping Witherspoon alerted as to the exact timing of the raid.

Witherspoon, on February 25, 1993, told his friend Dan Mullony, a cameraman for television station KWTX, that something heavy was coming down at the Mt. Carmel Center. Mullony called his friend Darlene Helmstetter, a dispatcher for American Medical Transport Ambulances Service. She told him three ambulances had been placed on standby for Monday at the request of law enforcement. She would eventually tell Mullony the date had been moved up from March 1.

On Friday afternoon, at the site of a car accident, an AMT medic also told Mullony something big was coming down. John McLemore, a reporter for the Tribune-Herald, told patrons at a bar that the ATF was going to conduct a big raid the next day.

Who else knew of the date of the raid, God only knows. The day of the raid the convoy of 80 vehicles with their headlights on, and a cattle car at each end, arrived at the Bellmead Civic Center between 7:30 and 8:00a.m. The Civic Center is adjacent to a residential neighborhood and is visible from the nearby intersection of Interstate 84 and Loop 340, less than ten miles from the Mt. Carmel Center.

An ATF agent wearing an ATF raid jacket and local police were in the street in front of the Civic Center directing the convoy into the parking lot. Many agents, with their ATF insignias in full view, milled around outside the Civic Center, coffee and donuts close at hand. The three stooges would have been envious of the methods being employed to keep this raid "secret".

As has already been discussed earlier, ATF Order 1200.2B requires Washington Headquarters be notified where media ride-alongs are contemplated. The meeting that took place between Elmore, Dunagan, and Sarabyn in Bill Johnston's office, where the Tribune-Herald was offered "front row seats", was nothing less than a proposal for a ride-along.

The call to Elmore two weeks later, informing her of the changed date of the raid to March 1, 1993, was further confirmation that the Tribune-Herald would be foreseen to be a participant at the time the raid was contemplated. Chojnacki's invitation to Rochner, the paper's man in Atlanta, to observe ATF training at Fort Hood on February 26 and 27, buttress this argument completely.

On June 9, 1993, in a hearing before a sub-committee of The Committee on Appropriations, House of Representatives, headed by Steny H. Hoyer of Maryland, this subject was broached. Following are excerpts from those hearings.

Mr. Pasco. "I am the Assistant Director For Congressional And Media Affairs, and I thank you for the opportunity to discuss our public affairs policy and practices.

ATF policy recognizes that, as a publicly funded agency, we have an obligation to operate in as open a posture as possible, given legal and operational constraints. Our emphasis has always been on the safe performance of our duties, with press coverage as a secondary consideration. Nonetheless, for accountability and deterence, we believe it is entirely appropriate that through the media, the public has access to information concerning the ATF's missions and performance.

We train all of our senior managers and public information officers during a one-week media relations course. That course covers our policy, Department of Justice Policy, laws governing the release of information and sessions with media professionals. With regard to media coverage of actual enforcement operations, we instruct the media, generally, that they have a right to be where we would allow the general public to be.

We emphasize that planning for media coverage should be a part of operational planning. Whether or not to organize the media beforehand, or notify them after an operation, is based on the safety and integrity of the operation. We have certainly had requests from the media to accompany us on operations, and we have, in the past, accomodated them from time to time, with no negative impact on the operation or on the investigation.

However, that issue is not truly relevant to Waco. It was clearly recognized by us from the beginning that this was a high-risk operation and that the press itself was likely to be an inflammatory presence. Therefore, no media was allowed to accompany us on this raid. OUR DECISION WAS TO NOTIFY MEDIA OF THE OPERATION ONLY AFTER ITS CONCLUSION. Thank you."

And thank you Mr. Pasco, for taking the

sledgehammer out of my forehead so I can believe you.

Congressman Istook: "I did want to be clear. I think you covered this before regarding the press. Did I understand correctly that you indicated that no members of the media, to your knowledge, were advised in advance of the raid by anyone within the ATF or associated with the ATF?"

Director Stephen Higgins: "No, no representative of the ATF alerted the press in any way with respect to the raid."

And of course, last but not least, in this parade of pathological liars, Sharon Wheeler.

I truly believe Sharon Wheeler was set up to take the heat, once the mission would go awry. Chojnacki, the agent in charge of the Waco raid, had earlier requested Jack Killorin, Chief of ATF's Public Affairs Branch, handle the public information part of the raid, but was turned down by Pasco. Pasco claimed Killorin was needed in Washington D.C. (maybe they knew the World Trade Center was on tap and Killorin would be needed in New York. Just speculating) (Source: Treasury Department Report On Waco).

The only body still available was Wheeler. She was ordered by SAC Royster, her supervisor and one of the few remaining agents-in-charge of raid planning that hadn't talked to the Tribune-Herald directly, to call the Dallas media two days prior to the raid, and give them a hint.

Wheeler addressed the Appropriations Committee Hearing with an opening statement.

Ms. Wheeler: "Thank you very much. Mr. Chairman and members of the Subcommittee. First, I want to thank you for this opportunity to discuss my role in the Waco operation, and to finally set the record straight about what I did and did not do.

I was first advised of the Waco operation that I would be assigned to it several weeks before the operation was scheduled to occur. My assignment would be to work with press upon completion of the raid and to coordinate the media once they arrived in the Waco area.

Let me emphasize that we had no plan to advise the media about specific operations prior to the raid and that I did not do so and did not invite or arrange for any media to accompany us on the raid."

Wheeler goes on to admit she did contact the Dallas media as previously mentioned. And the above statement is probably true. Wheeler didn't need to contact the Waco media, it had already been done for her, and she could claim she didn't know and probably be telling the truth.

So what are we to make of all this? If our public servants such as U.S. Attorney Bill Johnston, Chuck Sarabyn, and Phil Chojnacki, had calculated and wanted the media on the scene as the raid took place, they, so far, have succeeded in remaining unaccountable for the lives that were lost as a result of the Davidians having knowledge the agents were on their way.

If the mucky-mucks in Washington D.C. were

calculating and had foreknowledge of the media being coordinated as part of the operation, they too, have escaped accountability. I submit to you that these men involved at the highest levels, including Chojnacki, Sarabyn, Dunagan, Killorin, Pasco, and Cox Enterprises man in Atlanta, Charles Rochner, are men of much greater intelligence and are involved with the shaping of the political landscape in much deeper ways than we currently grasp.

AMERIKAN HELICOPTERS MEET

SAMSON---THE 90'S VERSION

With but few exceptions, no definite time logs were ever recorded underlining events that would transpire on raid day.

From the undercover house that had been set up on January 11, 1993, Jim Cavanaugh, Assistant Special-Agent-In-Charge of the Dallas Office, watched the Mt. Carmel Center the morning of the raid. He was looking for any signs of unusual activity.

He saw nothing unusual. A few men walking around the grounds, some women doing daily chores.

ATF Agent Robert Rodriquez, one of the undercover agents living across the street and engaging in Bible studies with Koresh, entered the Mt. Carmel Center around 8:00 a.m. Two other agents were available to give Rodriquez back-up. Another of these undercover agents would bring snipers into a haybarn located behind the Center. Once the raid teams had exited the staging area in Waco, an undercover agent would alert the residents of the neighboring house to remain inside their dwelling during the raid.

At least this eight-man team sounded organized on raid day. But during the almost six weeks Chojnacki allocated this eight-man team to surveil and gather information on the Davidians residing at Mt. Carmel, their performance was anything but organized. Calling this team "undercover" is laughable.

The day this team moved in claiming they were students at the local technical college, they were visited by Davidians Wayne Martin (the lawyer), David Jones, and Neil Schroeder. Even though claiming to be students, Robert Rodriquez was over 40 years old when this assignment began.

Originally this team was to do around-the-clock surveillance of the Center. They were to determine if an armed guard or watch was maintained, to identify, count, and photograph Davidian members and their cars, to identify any counter-intelligence surveilling, and attempt to obtain any additional information involving further firearms violations.

Other than these delineations, this team of agents weren't given any solid sense of what information the tactical planners were seeking, nor were they made aware of the evolving tactical plan.

During the first eight days these agents were vigilant, keeping around-the-clock surveillance. However, due to lack of supervision and direction, this vigilance dissipated.

The agents in this "undercover" house communicated with the tactical planners through providing logs, photos, and video-cassettes to their contact agent. Though the agents allegedly took hundreds of photos of the Center and its residents, and also filmed hours of video, <u>NONE</u> of it was utilized by the tactical planners. Many of the photos weren't developed until long after the raid.

The agents couldn't even figure out how the pole-camera worked, and on January 21, it had to be removed due to a security leak by a power company employee (no, his name wasn't Ernest). Agent Spoons told agents on January 18, that Koresh thought the Center was being watched and expected to get a visit from the FBI.

Detective Closeau would have been proud, never mind envious, of this pack of "detective dorks" falling all over themselves to be the first one to shoot himself in the foot.

Adding insult to injury, apparently they couldn't count. This team reported 75 Davidians living in the Center. The fact is 127 people are present on raid day.

At 8:00 a.m. Chuck Sarabyn gives a short briefing at the Civic Center. He reviews the assignments of the various groups, alludes to the "Sinful Messiah" series that was published the day before, and gives Rodriquez's assessment of the "vibes" in the Center Saturday (yesterday).

He also hands out a photo of the most recent view of the Center and answers questions from team leaders. Sarabyn tells the assembly Rodriquez is in the Mt. Carmel Center and there will be a final briefing once Rodriquez reports back about currently existing conditions in the Center. Sarabyn then leaves the Civic Center for the TSTC Command Post, directly hooked up to the undercover house.

Activity at the TSTC Command Post began at dawn. Agent Lewis, in charge of logistics support, checked all the phones hooked to the undercover house. The three helicopters, one UH-60 Blackhawk and two OH-58 Jet Rangers, were on the tarmac.

Andy Vita, Chief of Firearms Division,

opened the ATF's National Command Center in Washington D.C., at 9:00 a.m.(EST). Richard Garner, Chief of the Special Operations Division; John Jensen, in charge of the National Communications Branch, and others designated by the National Response Plan, were also present. Director Stephen Higgins, Associate Director Daniel Hartnett, and Deputy Assistant Daniel Conroy were available by telephone.

As the ATF was amassing its considerable resources to embark on the assault, local reporters were gathering to cover the operation. At 7:00 a.m., KWTX had Jim Peeler, John McLemore, and Dan Mullony receive maps of the area and review assignments with the station's news director, Rick Bradfield. Bradfield knew this raid would be a heavy scene because he had learned through AMT Ambulance Service informant Darlene Helmstetter, that Careflight, a Fort-Worth based trauma flight company, would be available for service.

Peeler was sent to the intersection of Double E Ranch and Old Mexia roads where, according to Mullony, Peeler was to watch for, and film, raid helicopters. Peeler won't cop to this responsibility. I don't blame him. There has been numerous reports of those copters shooting into the roof of the Mt. Carmel Center that day. Various injuries to Davidians, including children, have been reported by various witnesses to the event. And review of the film that has been released, always cuts away when copters are focused on.

Prior to the raid, nine Tribune-Herald reporters were assigned to cover the developing story. The morning of the raid, some of them gathered at the newspaper's office. Three cars of Tribune reporters headed for the Mt. Carmel Center, a fourth car headed for the TSTC command post to keep an eye on the helicopters.

At about 7:30 a.m., after passing the Mt. Carmel Center twice, Dan Mullony parked on FR 2491 Rd. about one mile north of its intersection with Double E Ranch Rd. By 8:00 a.m., other Tribune-Herald vehicles were patrolling the two roads adjacent to the Center. At 9:30 a.m., Mark England, the author of the "Sinful Messiah" series, was on the road near the Center (Source: The Treasury Department Report On Waco).

While Robert Rodriquez, one of the undercover agents, was in the Center just prior to the raid, he said Perry Jones told Koresh there was a call from England.

This seems too coincidental to be merely pawned off as happenstance. Perry Jones could have used any name to get Koresh out of the room to relay his tip about the impending raid to Koresh, why use England's name?

In the hour before the raid, five media vehicles could be seen driving or parked on roads near the Center. The agents stationed in the undercover house reported the deluge to Agent Cavanaugh, but he wouldn't confirm or deny whether he alerted the Command Center.

While other reporters were waiting for the action to begin, KWTX cameraman Peeler, allegedly became lost. At about 8:30 a.m., he called Mullony by cellular phone and asked directions. Mullony was no help and about this time David Jones, a mail-carrier driving a vehicle with "U.S. Mail" painted on the door, pulled up and asked if Peeler was lost.

During the ensuing conversation Peeler

warned Jones not to go near the Center, as there was going to be a shoot-out with "60 to 70 men and helicopters raiding the place."

While Jones made a beeline for the Center, Peeler drove to a nearby store and contacted KWTX news director Rick Bradford. Bradford told Peeler to return to the scene. Upon Peeler's return, police had set up roadblocks and wouldn't let him pass. They did show Peeler where he could set up his camera, the camera missing so much footage.

Upon Jones arrival from his conversation with Peeler, David Jones allegedly relayed the Peeler conversation to his father, Perry Jones. It is alleged that Perry Jones called Koresh away from Rodriquez and told him of the impending raid.

When Koresh returned to the room, Rodriquez claims Koresh was visibly shaken, had trouble talking, and couldn't hold onto his Bible. Rodriquez asked him what was wrong. Rodriquez recalls that Koresh proclaimed, "Neither the ATF nor the National Guard will ever get me. They got me once and they'll never get me again."

Rodriquez said Koresh walked to a window and looked out, saying, "They're coming, Robert, the time has come." Koresh turned, looked at Rodriquez and repeated, "They're coming, Robert, they're coming."

Rodriquez claims he was shocked. Rodriquez wondered whether the raid was going to begin with him inside the Center. Needing an excuse to leave, Rodriquez told Koresh he was late for a breakfast date. Other Davidians came into the room placing themselves between Rodriquez and the door.

Rodriquez became frightened and contemplated jumping through the window. He repeated that he had to leave for a breakfast appointment.

Koresh approached him in what Rodriquez said was highly uncharacteristic behavior for Koresh, reached out and shook his hand, and said, "Good luck, Robert." Rodriquez left and drove his pick-up directly to the undercover house.

Awaiting agents said Rodriquez was visibly shaken when he entered the undercover house, complaining the windows in the house were raised and he could visibly see a camera in one of them.

Cavanaugh asked Rodriquez what was going on inside the Center. He told Cavanaugh that Koresh knew the ATF and the National Guard were on their way. However, he said he neither saw any guns, nor heard anyone talking about guns.

Rodriquez then called Sarabyn at the TSTC Command Center, and told him what he had seen. Sarabyn asked him a list of pre-written questions provided by the tactical planners: Did you see any weapons? Was there a call to arms? Was anyone making preparations? Rodriquez answered no to all these questions.

Sarabyn then asked him what the people were doing when he left the Center. Rodriquez said they were praying.

Sarabyn then called the undercover house and Cavanaugh said he saw no activity at the Center. This should have alerted Sarabyn, even more convincingly, that the plan had been compromised. One key element was surprise, another was the need to have the men working in the pit, away from any weapons.

According to the agent nearest the action, neither of these elements was present (Source: The Treasury Department Report On Waco).

Sarabyn now moved quickly to the area where the helicopters were starting to warm up. There he conferred with Chojnacki and Royster. He related what Rodriquez had told him and, after a mere three minutes, it was decided to blaze a trail to the Mt. Carmel Center.

News of Rodriquez report spread rapidly among the ATF agents at the Command Post. Agents were heard yelling that Koresh knew they were coming. Numerous shouts of "show-time", ringed the environment, as if this event were a simulation of a Laker's basket-ball game, with Jack Nicholsen watching from the front row. Despicable!!

Agent Royster ran back to the Command Post, joined by Chojnacki, who then called the National Command Center in Washington D.C., and reported to Special Agent Jensen, responsible for the Center's communications. Whether Chojnacki told Jensen about Rodriquez's report, no one is willing to say.

Chojnacki then jumped in his helicopter and the entire pack headed for Mt. Carmel. Rodriquez arrived shortly after their departure and upon learning of their departure, became distraught, repeatedly asking how they could have proceeded after what he had told them.

Sarabyn arrived at the staging area at about 9:10 a.m. He was reportedly very hyped, telling anyone within earshot, "Get ready. They know we're coming. We're going to hit them now." We're no longer getting the flavor of a basketball game. Suddenly, its war.

There was no formal briefing, as was discussed earlier in the morning. Several agents had qualms about going forward since the element of surprise had been lost. Nonetheless, given the pressure of the moment, it was felt inappropriate to protest.

Within 15 minutes of Sarabyn's arrival, the Special Response and the Arrest teams had piled into the cattle trailers and departed. Sarabyn was in the first cattle trailer.

As the entourage headed for the Mt. Carmel Center, Sarabyn maintained an open line to Cavanaugh, by cellular phone, located at the undercover house. Cavanaugh told Sarabyn there was <u>NO</u> activity at the Center, nor anyone outside on its grounds.

According to Davidians exiting Mt. Carmel during the 51 day standoff, those inside the Center began arming themselves with a variety of weapons. But this arming didn't begin until almost an hour after Rodriquez exited the Center that morning.

The older women and children were directed to the second floor where they were to lie down, away from the outer walls. Other Davidians assumed positions at various windows, ready to defend themselves.

Upon entry into the grounds of Mt. Carmel, the approaching agents noted the lack of activity inside or outside the Center. Over their radios one agent spoke to another, "There's no one outside." The second agent responded, "That's not good."

The cattle trailers arrived in a burst

of speed in front of the main building. What happened next depends on who you talk to and what you believe. After all, this still is, even at this late date, America.

We can talk, cajole, argue, debate, dispute, doing all manner of analysis of what occurred during this shoot-out, and we still part company believing what we <u>think</u> happened, depending on our perspective.

The Treasury Department Report On Waco gives a sequence of events from the ATF perspective. The authors of the report claim to have taken extensive interviews with the participants, analyzed numerous photographs, examined autopsy records, and so forth. Their version follows:

The trucks stopped in front of the Compound's main building as planned. Agents with fire extinguishers for holding the Compound's dogs at bay were the first to exit the trailer. One agent opened the gate in the wall in front of the Compound, and another discharged a fire extinguisher at the dogs. Simultaneously, agents began exiting the second trailer. Koresh appeared at the front door and yelled, "What's going on?"

The agents identified themselves, stated they had a warrant and yelled, "freeze" and "get down". But Koresh slammed the door before agents could get to it. Gunfire from inside the Compound burst through the door. The force of the gunfire was so great that the door bowed outward. The agent closest to the door was shot in the thumb before he could dive for cover into a pit near the door. Then gunfire erupted from virtually every window in the front of the Compound. The Dallas and Houston Special Response teams, which were approaching the front of the Compound and the pit area to the left, took the brunt of the initial barrage. Agents scrambled for cover. One of the first shots fired hit the engine block of the lead pick-up truck, the one Sarabyn was in. Consequently, neither the first, nor the second vehicle were able to leave.

As the Dallas and Houston teams attempted to get to the front of the Compound, the New Orleans team, which had been concealed in the second trailer, approached the east side of the Compound. As they left the trailer, the agents heard gunfire. At first, the agents thought it came from the dog teams. During training the agents had been told that they might hear the dog teams firing at the dogs if they were not able to subdue them with fire extinguishers. However, they quickly realized that the gunfire was coming from the Compound. While one agent provided cover from the ground, seven others approached the wall and climbed to the roof. Conway Lebleu, Todd McKeehan, Kenny King, and David Millen were to enter Koresh's bedroom on the west pitch of the roof, while Bill Buford, Keith Constantino and Glen Jordan were to enter the window on the east pitch of the roof. That window led to the room that ATF intelligence indicated contained the weapons. But soon after the agents reached the roof, they came under heavy gunfire. Special Agent Millen was able to retreat back to the east pitch of the roof where he stood guard outside the armory. Special Agent Lebleu and Special Agent McKeehan were killed.

Special Agent King was shot six times before managing to roll himself off the roof and into the courtyard behind the Compound. As he lay trapped in the courtyard, too injured to move, King repeatedly called over his radio that he had been shot several times and was bleeding badly. Agents hearing King's pleas, tried to rescue him. New Orleans Field Division SAC, Pete Mastin, contacted Cavanaugh and asked whether the forward observers could suppress fire from the tower while agents on the ground attempted to rescue King. The forward observers directed rifle fire at the area of the tower from which shots had been directed at the agents. However, as the agents attempted to move toward the rear of the Compound, gunfire from other areas stopped them. Despite the agents' best efforts, the intensity of the gunfire made it impossible to rescue King until the final cease-fire, approximately an hour and a half later.

At the arms room, Agent Jordan managed to "break and rake" the window and Agent Buford threw a distraction device into the room. Buford, Constantino and Jordan entered. Inside, Agent Buford saw a person armed with an assault rifle backing out a doorway, in the far left corner of the room. That individual began firing into the room from the other side of the thin walls. The agents returned fire, but without automatic weapons, which are used to deliver a defensive spray of gunfire, they could not suppress the attacker's fire. The shots fired at the agents inside the room passed through the wall where Special Agent Millen was positioned on the roof. Shots were also fired at Millen from the first floor up through the roof. He escaped the attacks by sliding down the ladder to the ground.

Inside the room, Buford was shot twice

in the upper thigh. Agent Constantino provided cover for Buford and Jordan while they ran back for the window, dove onto the pitched roof and then dropped to the ground. As Agents Chisolm and Bonaventure dragged Buford out of the line of fire, they were fired upon. A bullet creased Buford's nose. Agent Chisolm threw his body over Buford to protect him. When the shooting stopped, Chisolm and Bonaventure pulled Buford to a safe position. Chisolm, the medic for his team, observed Buford's wounds and began administering an IV to him.

Immediately after Buford and Jordan were out of the arms room, the firing stopped. As Constantino was deciding whether to hold his position or make a run for the window, a cult member entered the room aiming an assault rifle at him. He fired two or three shots at Constantino. Constantino returned fire and the man fell. Constantino ran for the window, but as he was going through it, he struck his head, knocked off his helmet and dropped his weapon. Dazed, he rolled off the roof and fell to the ground, severely fracturing his hip and leg and causing extensive injury to both knees. As he lay on the ground, vulnerable to the cult's guns, he saw two agents who had taken cover near the wall of the Compound. Constantino put his hand out and Special Agents David Millen and Charles Smith dragged him out of the line of fire (contrary to some publicly disseminated accounts, none of the agents that entered the armory were killed).

Special Agents Steven C. Willis and Robert J. Williams were killed during the ambush. Agent Willis, a member of the Houston raid support team, had taken cover behind a van parked near the right front corner of the

Compound. Special Agent Williams, New Orleans SRT, was providing cover for his teammates mounting the roof. Intense gunfire forced him to seek cover behind a large metal object on the ground to the east side of the Compound.

Throughout the vicious firefight, ATF agents demonstrated extraordinary discipline and courage. Special agents Bernadette Griffin, Jonathan Zimmer and Martin Roy were pinned down behind a shed when Special Agent Jordan, who had been wounded in the arms room, staggered over to where they were and collapsed on them. Special Agent Griffin discovered that Jordan's arm was bleeding profusely. She elevated his arm and compressed the wound with her hand until the cease-fire, 90 minutes later. Special Agent Chisolm, relinquished his own protected location, came to their location and rendered medical aid. Special Agent Tim Gabourie, a medic with the Dallas SRT, who also repeatedly exposed himself to gunfire to treat several wounded agents, had one of his medical bags shot out of his hand by .50-caliber gunfire (Writer's note: at trial evidence showed that only <u>one</u> .50-caliber shell casing was found in the rubble after the fire, and it hadn't been fired). He braved gunfire in an unsuccessful effort to reach Special Agent Willis who died during the battle.

In the face of insurmountable, unrelenting automatic and semi-automatic weapons fire from virtually every area of the Compound, the agents had no choice but to remain in their covered positions. The openness of the terrain made retreat impossible. They returned fire when possible, but conserved their ammunition. They also fired only when they saw an individual engaged in a threatening action, such as pointing a weapon. Neither of these constraints applied to those in the Branch Davidian Compound who had virtually limitless supply of ammunition (several hundred thousand rounds of ammunition were later found in the Compound) and could fire at will. They even fired at the undercover house and at the reporters parked on the road in front of the Compound (Writer's note: film footage shows ATF agents beating up a cameraman on raid day).

In addition to the agent fatalities, the cult's weapons inflicted vicious wounds on other agents. For example, one agent was shot in both legs by a shotgun. Another agent was shot in the left leg by one bullet while a second passed through his left leg and lodged in his right leg. There were many other serious wounds and related injuries.

In contrast to the extensive casualties inflicted upon the agents, there were few casualties among the cult members. Autopsies revealed that two cult members were killed by agents in the entry teams returning fire. Autopsies of two other cult fatalities reveal that they were shot at close range: Perry Jones was killed by a shot in his mouth, a manner of death consistant with suicide; Peter Hipsman was wounded but was later killed by a cult member who shot him at close range in the back of his skull---an apparent mercy killing, although the autopsy revealed that his initial wound would not have been fatal. Koresh was wounded both in the pelvic area and in his wrist.

According to McLennan County 911 records,

Branch Davidian Wayne Martin called the Waco 911 emergency service at 9:48. His call was handled by Deputy Larry Lynch. Martin sounded very frightened and Lynch heard gunfire in the background. Deputy Lynch attempted to speak with Martin, but Martin did not respond and at 10:02, Martin hung up (Writer's note: the tape played at the trial shows Martin is in communication with Lynch when unknown sources disconnect them. Lynch and the Davidians were disconnected numerous times).

Using the telephone number that appears on a screen when a call is placed to 911, Lynch called back to the Compound. An answering machine responded. Hoping that Martin, or someone in the Compound, could hear, Lynch yelled for Martin to pick up the phone. Martin responded and Lynch began attempting to arrange a cease-fire. Simultaneously, Lynch tried to contact ATF through Lieutenant Barber, who as the liason between ATF and the Sheriff's Department, was at the Command Post. However, Barber had turned off his radio because he was planning to assist the bomb technicians in recovering and processing any explosives. Although Lynch was unable to raise ATF on his radio, a TSTC officer, Jim Stone, responded and said that he was able to contact ATF. Stone drove to the Command Post and reached SAC Chojnacki. Chojnacki used Stone's radio to speak with Deputy Lynch.

Afraid that if Martin was told to hang up the telephone to allow ATF to contact him directly, contact might not be restored, ATF worked through Lynch. Thus, Martin was in contact with Deputy Lynch, who had to relay what Martin said to Chojnacki by way of Stone's radio. Lynch told Martin to cease firing while simultaneously arranging for ATF agents at the Compound to do the same and pull back.

At 10:34, Martin advised Deputy Lynch that someone else in the Compound wanted to speak to Lynch. At 10:35 Koresh called Lynch. Lynch was then in contact with Martin on one telephone line, David Koresh on another, and ATF by radio, as he attempted to arrange a cease-fire. The negotiations were unproductive, stymied by the unwieldy communications and confusion in the Compound.

In the undercover house, Cavanaugh eventually decided that the Sheriff's Department was not making sufficient progress toward achieving a cease-fire, but he did not have the telephone number for any phone in the Compound. He yelled across to the agents in the neighboring house, who yelled back that the number was on the refrigerator. Cavanaugh found the number and dialed the Compound. The phone rang repeatedly but no one answered the telephone. Cavanaugh found it necessary to radio agents on the Compound grounds to yell into the Compound for someone to answer the phone. Then, Branch Davidian Steve Schneider answered the telephone. Cavanaugh identified himself and told Schneider that he wanted to discuss the situation. Through the telephone Cavanaugh could hear yelling, screaming, and crying in the Compound. Intermittent gunfire between agents and those in the Compound punctuated the intense standoff. Schneider was frantic and hostile. It took Cavanaugh several minutes to calm him. When Cavanaugh began to discuss arranging a cease-fire, Schneider was receptive because individuals in the Compound had also been wounded. But even after Schneider and Cavanaugh had agreed to call a cease-fire, it took several minutes to achieve one. Schneider for his part, had to walk throughout the

Compound to tell people inside to stop shooting. Cavanaugh, who had no direct link by radio to each agent, had to advise the team leaders of the cease-fire and the team leaders in turn had to communicate with their agents. The cease-fire was negotiated for a period of time before the shooting finally stopped.

The cease-fire agreement did not address how the agents would leave. Cavanaugh told Schneider that ATF wanted to retrieve its dead and wounded agents. Schneider demanded that the agents withdraw unconditionally. Cavanaugh insisted that the agents would leave only if they could retrieve their wounded and dead. Schneider who remained excitable and irrational insisted that the agents would leave immediately. Cavanaugh assured Schneider that the agents would retreat, but vowed not without their fallen comrades. Retrieval of King, who had fallen in the rear courtyard, was a particularly difficult point of negotiation. Initially, Schneider would not allow agents to go to the courtyard for King. Cavanaugh was able to discuss with Schneider King's precise location, even arranging for Schneider to have someone in the Compound look in the courtyard to verify that the agent was there. Eventually, Schneider agreed to let agents retrieve King.

Cavanaugh instructed the agents to raise their hands, not make any sudden movements and begin leaving the grounds. At approximately 11:34, SAC Mastin approached Agents Griffin, Bonaventure, and Chisolm to assist them in retrieving King from the rear courtyard. When they reached the courtyard area, they began searching for King. Suddenly, one of the Branch Davidians aimed a rifle at Griffin and yelled racial slurs at her.

Griffin decided that if she was going to be shot, she would rather it be while attempting to assist one of her fellow agents. She turned and walked toward King. The cult member did not shoot.

King was too seriously injured to be carried without a stretcher, so the agents placed him on a ladder. They brought him out to the front of the Compound and put him in an ambulance that Special Agents Aguilera and Dunagan had driven to the Compound, with Special Agent Rodriquez and Agent Salas riding in the back to provide assistance. The AMT driver was not present because ATF could not guarantee his safety.

By this time, most of the agents able to walk had gathered near a large bus to the right of the Compound. At 11:46 Cavanaugh was able to persuade Schneider to allow the ATF to retrieve the remaining dead and wounded agents. The cease-fire left the agents at a significant tactical disadvantage. The agents were not covered, while the cult members were shielded inside the Compound's main building with vantage points on floors above the ground. While many agents were almost out of ammunition, the Branch Davidians were well supplied, which became clear when the Compound was searched after the April 19 fire. Under the threat of Branch Davidian gunfire, the agents withdrew, some with holstered weapons, some with their shields raised, some with their hands in the air, and some with their backs to the Compound. The dead agents and those unable to walk, were placed in any available vehicle: the ambulance; a pickup truck that had been parked in front of the undercover house; and a KWTX reporter's Ford Bronco. The six agents in the undercover house, rearranged the furniture into a defensive configuration and the forward observers monitored the retreat, prepared to return fire if necessary. The agents stayed in the undercover house until later that afternoon, when they received support from the Texas Department of Public Safety SWAT team who took positions at the nearby roadblock. At roughly the same time, ATF agents who had taken positions in a building near the undercoverhouse were also able to withdraw safely. During the cease-fire, some agents had moved from the hay barn closer to the Compound. From this relatively safe, high ground, they had an excellent view of the Compound. But soon they were ordered back to the hay barn where they had no such vantage point.

Because no one had designed a rallying point at which agents would take a defensive position, or had ordered a sequential withdrawal that might have permitted some agents to cover movements of others, the retreat continued until agents reached the roadblock at the intersection of Double E Road and FM2491. There, arrangements were made for bus transportation, first to a nearby social club, the Pep Club, and then back to the staging area. It was approximately 1:00 p.m. when the withdrawal negotiations were completed. Once the agents had left the Compound grounds, Cavanaugh agreed with Schneider that no agents would come on the property, and no one inside would attempt to leave. Cavanaugh told Schneider that he would call again at 2:00 p.m. Cavanaugh then arranged for the residents of the neighboring house to be taken to a hotel, and he went to the Command Post.

There you have it. The government's version. In the aftermath of the Waco assault, the Treasury Department promised a full and complete report of the events that transpired before, during and after the raid on Mt. Carmel. When the report came out in September of 1993, it was titled, "Report of THE DEPARTMENT OF THE TREASURY on the BUREAU OF ALCOHOL, TOBACCO, AND FIREARMS Investigation of Vernon Wayne Howell also known as David Koresh." Even the title betrays the mission.

Were the Branch Davidians and David Koresh deserving of the government's placing them at the top of its most pressing priority list of subversives? On balance, the Davidians appear to be nothing more than a rather remote, rag-tag bunch of southerners, looking more like the Beverly Hillbillies after being touched "by the Holy Ghost." Was this really a legitimate government operation the ATF chose to engage in? Or were there other, more pressing reasons to place Waco, Texas, high on the Treasury Department's priority list?

LOOK, ITS HALLEY'S COMET!

On February 26, 1993, at 12:18 p.m. an enormous explosion ripped apart the basement floor of the World Trade Center building in New York City. This explosion ripped a 180'-by-12' hole in a wall above an underground train station, creating a 200'-by-100' crater in the garage below the Center's Vista Hotel.

The Hotel's first floor was totally destroyed, and the building suffered severe structural damage. Dust and smoke reached up as high as the 96th floor in the 110-story twin towers (Source: Target America, by Bodansky).

After the ATF went over the scene with a fine tooth comb, the inspectors concluded that only an expert would know where to place such a bomb, how much explosives to use, and how to place such a device to achieve maximum damage. The ATF speculates that the intent was to collapse one tower into the other, destroying both towers for the price of one.

Upon closer scrutiny, we discover Assistant Director and Head of the FBI's office in New York City, James Fox, was only two blocks from the Twin Towers when the explosion occurred. Fox didn't even hail a cab, he could walk to the scene. Had both towers been brought down by the explosion, Fox would have remained unscathed, two blocks being the minimum distance needed for safety.

As an Assistant Director, Fox is part of the FBI's executive conference, the top executives who meet on Thursday mornings at headquarters in Washington D.C. to plan strategy. That gives the head of the New York office more access to top FBI officials than the chiefs of other field offices.

It was revealed on "60 Minutes" that law enforcement was in possession of a notebook detailing plans to bomb various structures, including the World Trade Center, as early as 1990. The notebook was allegedly written by one of the suspects scheduled to go on trial in November of 1994 (Source: Mike Wallace, "60 Minutes", November 13, 1994).

James Fox, as Head of the New York Office, was in charge of counterintelligence and criminal cases. Traditionally, the FBI's office has devoted as much as half of its manpower to counterintelligence cases (Source: "The FBI, by Ron Kessler). Yet the FBI's Buck Revell claims the FBI didn't read the notebook detailing plans for bombing missions in New York City.

Just who the hell is Buck Revell? A career FBI man with an M.A. from Temple University, Buck acted as the Marine laison with the FBI on Lee Harvey Oswald's record in the Marines after John Kennedy was shot.

Buck was placed in charge of federal law enforcement in Los Angeles, including law enforcement activities of the military (the military that forget to bring any bullets), during the Los Angeles riots. He was placed there by Attorney General William Barr. I'll get to Barr later.

And as SAC of the Dallas office, Revell participated in the plan to gas the Davidians with CS gas that resulted in the April 19, 1993, fire and frying of those inside Mt. Carmel.

As a career agent, Revell has helped develop policy and serve on a dizzying array of interagency and international committees that deal with intelligence counterintelligence, terrorism, and so forth. Under Revell, the FBI built its operations center, known as SIOC, and started a hostage rescue team, the one doing the evil deeds for 51 days to those inside Mt. Carmel. Yes, Buck Revell, there's more here than meets the eye, and volumes meet the eye. (Source: "The FBI", by Ronald Kessler).

The World Trade Center bombing killed six people and injured over one-thousand. Monetary damage exceeded $600 million. The World Trade Center was Amerika's first experience with foreign terrorists operating on Amerikan soil. The level of fear and paranoia within New York City was unprecedented.

No one was really certain if the World Trade Center bombing was the beginning of a nationwide attack on our nation's large cities by foreign terrorists. The bombing heavily damaged Secret Service and U.S. Customs facilities, raising concerns within the Office of Enforcement of the Treasury Department over possible injuries to Secret Service and Customs personnel.

Ronald Noble, President Clinton's designee to head the Office of the Assistant Secretary For Enforcement (and one of the parties that initially gave thumbs down to the ATF's planned Waco raid), was enroute by train to New York City from Washington D.C. when informed of the ATF failure in Waco.

Noble sought the advice of FBI Assistant Director Floyd Potts and Deputy Director Floyd

Clark. Apparently, these men were concerned that the World Trade Center might prove to be the beginning of a much larger terrorist plot. Remember the notebook in James Fox possession. These men, along with Acting Attorney General Stuart Gerson, remained at the FBI Command Center in Washington D.C., the day Waco was raided (Source: The Treasury Department Report On Waco, page 114,178).

So within 48 hours, Amerikans experienced their first foreign terrorist attack and the largest civilian law enforcement activity in U.S. history. In shear dollars and cents, the World Trade Center bombing and related lost revenue, is estimated to be at least 100 times more costly than Waco, costing at least $600 million.

Yet, the Waco raid took command of the front page of every major newspaper in the country. Whether by design or happenstance, the events in Waco moved the mainstream media's magnifying glass from New York City, to Nowhere, Texas.

And as we have all learned by the recent media blitz revolving around the O.J. Simpson case, when the media focus on an event and are left unrestrained, none of us get any respite until the last stone has been overturned.

Had Waco never occurred, what would we have learned about the World Trade Center bombing that would have perked our nation up? If blue collar workers didn't have Koresh and his 15 wives to discuss over morning coffee, what would they have been discussing about the Trade Center bombing once the media deluge began?

The date of the bombing has significance. Exactly two years to the day prior to the bombing, Iraq was forced to exit Kuwait City. Amerika opened the book, that glorious book on Desert Storm. Or should it have been called Desert Burial?

Conservative estimates have us using giant caterpillars to overcome the so-called crack Iraqi Republican Army that had burrowed under the sand on the Iraq-Kuwait border, burying upwards of 200,000 Iraqis alive. Testing our "smart weapons" on Iraq's infrastructure, and literally bombing them back to the stone age.

Had Waco not garnered most of the media focus, we might have gotten more details about how Iraq was assisted during the Reagan and Bush administrations through clandestined banking arrangements, to build its military into the fourth most powerful on earth.

Details of how these administrations helped finance the Iraqi military buildup have been recorded by none other than a man whose congressional offices were located less than a block from where 11 Branch Davidians were required to play kangaroos in a courtroom proceeding charging them with murder, among other charges. I'm referring to Henry Gonzalez, Chairman of the House Banking Committee, and as of this writing, heading the House side of the Whitewater hearings.

Ole Henry has spoken on the House floor on at least 33 separate occasions between 1990-1994, having his findings published in the Congressional Record showing in detail, the unlawful activities engaged in by members of the Bush and Reagan teams. The most despicable acts being the failure to act on behalf of the Amerikan public by Bush Administration

Justice Department officials.

Gonzalez details in the Congressional Record how foreign banks were able to make federally insured loans through various federal loan programs such as the Agriculture Department Commodities Credit Corporation and the related Export-Import Bank.

Particularly galling was Gonzalez factual analysis of the Banca Nazionale del Lavoro (a bank owned exclusively by the Italian government) and its link to Iraq's military procurement network, a very intricate, a very astute, and very infinitely thought-out procurement network.

To quote the July 21, 1992, Congressional Record by Gonzalez concerning the Bush Administration's Iraqi military buildup:

"When we talk about state enterprises, there is nothing else in those countries. The same man who is the Minister of Procurement and Economic Development, is the man in charge of defense procurement, and in one case there, and for awhile, it happened to be Saddam Hussein's relative.

High-speed photography gear for work on projectile behavior, for instance, and terminal ballistics was approved because, and I quote, 'This equipment is appropriate for conventional artillery rounds but far too slow for nuclear application.'

In short, the policy was to let Iraq have goods that could easily be used or diverted to nuclear applications with a request that Saddam Hussein refrain from doing so.

This occurred despite the fact that everyone concerned knew that Saddam Hussein was making every effort to develop nuclear weapons.

This occurred despite ample knowledge of Hussein's ruthless brutality, **and this** occurred despite knowledge that the threat was real, it was serious, and it was ongoing.

The truth is that the United States did nothing to check how the United States technology was used in Iraq.

Out of 771 export licenses granted Iraq, only one was ever checked to ensure that the equipment was actually being used for civilian purposes, only one out of 771.

So when the President claims, and I am going to quote his words, "We did not enhance Iraq's nuclear, biological, or chemical weapons and missile capabilities," it simply is contradictory to the facts as adduced in the evidence and in the documents that we are presenting to our colleagues.

What the President knew was that Saddam Hussein wanted nuclear weapons---there is no way to escape that conclusion---longrange, ballistic missiles, and chemical and biological weapons, and that he had an elaborate plan to get them."

That was Henry Gonzalez on July 21, 1992. We have recently discovered that between 600,000-700,000 soldiers serving in the military during Desert Storm, may have been exposed to these biological and chemical weapons Gonzalez mentions above.

Dr. Ellen Silbergeld, a molecular toxicologist at the University of Maryland, told a congressional hearing in August of 1994, scientists know men exposed to toxic chemicals can pass the poison directly to their children through semen. What is frightening, she said, is the chemicals can cause genetic mutations to the sperm that helps conceive the child.

Dr. Francis J. Waickman, an Akron, Ohio, environmental pediatrician, compared birth defect statistics between Gulf War babies and other children. He found a 30 percent rate of abnormalities among the children of Gulf veterans--"probably tenfold of what is in the normal population," he said.

And in Waynesboro, Miss., site of a National Guard quartermaster corps., 13 of the 15 children born to returning Gulf War veterans suffer serious birth defects (Source: N.B.C. NOW, August 24, 1994). Of course, the federal government denies the problem is real. Where is Buck Revell when we really need him?

Gonzalez points out that law enforcement officials investigating U.S. firms involved in arming Iraq have complained of being denied adequate resources, have trouble getting export licensing information from the Commerce Department, and received scant assistance from the intelligence community until well after the Iraqi invasion of Kuwait.

And in a letter Gonzalez received and included in the Congressional Record July 31, 1992, by then CIA Director Robert Gates, concerning the repercussions Italy's Banco del Lavoro Nazionale's Atlanta branch scandal might have on Italy:

"The revelation that a U.S. branch of an Italian Bank, Banca Nazionale del Lavoro (BNL), granted more than 3 billion dollars in unauthorized letters of credit to Iraq has had wide-ranging repercussions for Iraq and Italy. For Iraq, public disclosure that it used some of the credits to acquire military-related technology has impeded procurement efforts, and the suspension of BNL credits has slowed civilian reconstruction and development projects. For Italy, the BNL scandal has cast at least a temporary shadow on Prime Minister Andreotti's new government, raised questions about public-sector enterprises and reopened the issue of privatization.

The Atlanta, Georgia branch of the state-owned Banca Nazionale del Lavoro (BNL), Italy's largest bank, extended $3.2 billion in 2,500 unauthorized letters of credit for Iraq between February 1988 and July 1989. U.S. and Italian authorities have been investigating the scandal since July for violations of banking regulations and tax and customs laws.

Fragmentary reporting indicates BNL-Atlanta disbursed $1.84 billion of the $3.2 billion, including at least $800 million in letters of credit guaranteed by the U.S. Commodity Credit Corporation (CCC). BNL headquarters agreed to release another $550 million in early October,---after Iraq threatened to suspend payment to Italian firms if the bank failed to honor its commitments.

BNL-Atlanta's unusual activities included:

Exceeding the branch's allowable debt of $500,000 per customer.

Charging Baghdad an average 0.2-percent commission instead of the usual 15 percent for a poor credit risk.

Financing the letters of credit by borrowing from other banks for 90 to 180 days but allowing Iraq up to five years to repay.

BNL's North American headquarters in New York, and the bank's directors in Rome, publicly denied knowing about the letters of credit, although a BNL official in Chicago claims he notified New York and Rome several times about the unusual activity in Atlanta, according to press reports. Press reports also indicate a BNL branch in Udine, Italy, referred customers exporting to Iraq, to the Atlanta branch. Iraqi officials have generally denied knowledge of any wrongdoing, arguing that Baghdad is a victim in the scandal.

The BNL affair, in combination with other scandals, has cast a shadow on Prime Minister Andreotti's three-month-old government. Partly to divert attention from the BNL affair (Writer's note: apparently Mr. Gates willingly acknowledges a government's willingness to manipulate its citizen's focus), the Socialists and some Christian Democrats are playing up other scandals, including renewed allegations that the Italian Military covered up evidence concerning the 1980 crash of an Italian airliner north of Sicily. None of the governing political parties or their factions, however, appears now to believe it can strengthen its relative positions by explaining the issue.

The discovery of BNL's exposure in Iraq forced the bank to seek funds to boost its capital, which the Bank of Italy already considered too low. If Iraq defaulted, BNL technically would have been bankrupt because the amount of its loans to Iraq exceeded the bank's capital. In that event, the Bank of Italy and the Treasury Ministry would have been compelled to bail out the bank. Rome was stymied in finding a Socialist-controlled institution to recapitalize the bank by itself, and the government, in October, finally cobbled together a $1.7 billion package from the Treasury, a state-owned insurance company, and the Social Security Fund, thus maintaining a Socialist majority on the BNL board of directors.

We believe the revelations of BNL's dealings with Iraq along with other recent scandals, stand in counterpoint to growing Italian self-confidence on the international stage in recent years. After more than three decades of international diffidence, we believe Italian leaders have been pursuing a diplomatic profile more commensurate with their country's international economic role. Italians have felt particular pride because:

Italian troops in the Beirut peacekeeping forces had fulfilled their mission as defined by Rome.

The Italian decision to accept U.S. Cruise missiles played a decisive role in swinging West Germany behind deployment.

Their country's GDP had surpassed that of the United Kingdom, and possibly France.

In the opinion of almost all Italian press commentators, the BNL affair had a negative impact on Italy's credibility throughout the West. We believe, however, that the setback to Rome's international standing has been substanially less than that portrayed in the Italian press, and we expect the scandal will gradually fade from public view within Italy and will have little lasting impact on the country's perception of its international role."

The above quoted CIA internal memorandum dated November 6, 1989, has some juicy insights into how governments operate behind closed doors.

It also raises some interesting questions. Since BNL is government owned, why was Italy so enamored with financing Iraq's military buildup?

Why was our Justice Department and Intelligence agencies willing participants in hiding facts and evidence?

Henry Kissinger, one of the best known and most powerful Presidential advisors of the post-war era, began his political career in 1956 as a consultant on military affairs. He advised many executive branch organizations including the Joint Chiefs of Staff, the National Security Council, and Department of State. In 1969, he became President Nixon's National Security Advisor, and in 1973, Nixon named him Secretary of State.

Kissinger remains active as a foreign policy analyst and consultant. In 1989, Mr. Kissinger was a member of the President's Foreign Intelligence Advisory Board. Members in this elite club are permitted access to highly classified information, and members actually advise the President directly on intelligence issues.

In 1982, Kissinger founded Kissinger Associates with offices in New York and Washington D.C. It is said that the firm analyzes political risk and international economic trends to help clients make concrete business decisions. Several of the Kissinger Associates clients are also members of the United States-Iraq Business Forum.

And the kicker: Henry Kissinger was a paid member of the Banca Nazionale del Lavoro Consulting Board For International Policy, earning $20,000 per board appearance. Mr.

Mr. Kissinger held this position during the height of the biggest banking scandal of all time (Source: House Banking Committee Chairman Henry Gonzalez).

Other former or current employees of Kissinger Associates had links to Iraq. Many Kissinger Associates clients received United States Export licenses for exports to Iraq. Several were also the beneficiaries of BNL loans to Iraq.

Lawrence Eagleburger, Deputy Secretary of State from 1989-1992, has held many positions of international influence, in both the private and public sectors. Eagleburger started his political career in 1957, as a Foreign Service Officer.

In 1969, Henry Kissinger became Nixon's National Security Advisor, and Eagleburger served as his executive assistant. After working as a political advisor to NATO in Belgium, and as Deputy Assistant Secretary in the Department of Defense, Eagleburger joined Kissinger at the State Department, again as his executive assistant in 1973. Eagleburger was appointed Ambassador to Yugo-Slavia during the Carter Administration and served in that capacity from 1977-1981. Eagleburger has remained a close ally of Yugoslavia, or what remains of Yugoslavia.

Before assuming the position of Deputy Secretary of State, Eagleburger served as President of Kissinger Associates.

During hearings to confirm Eagleburger, he identified a number of prominent clients of Kissinger Associates. Eagleburger was a director of ITT, Alcatel, Bethlehem Rebar, Global Motors, Mutual of New York, Josephson

International, and Best Mart. Mr. Eagleburger was director of LBS Bank from 1986-1990. LBS Bank is one of the largest banks in Yugoslavia.

Global Motors was the corporation established in the U.S. to distribute the Yugo, since gone bankrupt. The Yugoslavian maker of the Yugo is a firm called Zavodi Crevna Zastava (ZCZ). ZCZ is the backbone of the Yugoslavian arms industry and its main clients include Iraq, Libya, and other eastern European nations. At least this was the case until Yugoslavia engaged in civil war and its political structure fragmented. After Iraq, Yugoslavia was BNL's largest customer (Source: Congressional Record, April 25, 1991).

Another Kissinger Associates alumni is Brent Scowcroft, a career Air Force officer and a specialist in Slavic languages and history, who has held various positions in six administrations.

After earning a Ph.D. and working in academia from 1962-1968, he held a succession of national security posts in the Department of Defense. In 1971, Nixon appointed Scowcroft Military Aide to the President an in 1973, Kissinger chose him to be Deputy Assistant to the President for National Security Affairs.

Scowcroft often took charge of the National Security Council while Kissinger was fulfilling his duties as Secretary of State, and in 1975 succeeded Kissinger as National Security Advisor under President Ford. Although he resigned the position during the Carter administration, Scowcroft stayed active as member of the President's General Advisory Committee on Arms Control.

In 1982, Scowcroft joined Kissinger in setting up Kissinger Associates. Scowcroft served as vice-chairman until regaining his position as National Security Advisor to President Bush in 1989. You may recall Scowcroft, Edmund Muskie, and the late John Tower were appointed by the Reagan Administration to "investigate" Iran-Contra. The Tower Commission cleared the Reagan Administration of wrongdoing.

Mr. Scowcroft's financial disclosure forms indicate that up until October 4, 1990, he owned stock in 40 companies. Several of the companies, like Lockheed and General Electric, are among the nation's largest defense contractors. Other companies include multinationals like General Motors, ITT, Westinghouse, AT&T, Mobil Oil, Du Pont, Xerox, and Hewlett-Packard. All of these companies must obtain export licenses as a part of their international business operations.

The NSC has direct responsibility for carrying out the President's national security directives. In the case of export licensing, the National Security Act of 1947, and subsequent legislation provided the President, give the National Security Council (NSC) ample authority to establish policies on export controls.

And the kicker: companies that Mr. Scowcroft owned stock in received 100 out of the total 800 U.S. export licenses for sales to Iraq (Source: Congressional Record, April 25, 1991).

While at Kissinger Associates, Mr. Scowcroft worked on the BNL account and met on numerous occasions with the BNL management.

On three occasions between 1986 and 1989, Mr. Scowcroft briefed the BNL board on international political and economic developments. In addition, when the President of BNL traveled to the United States to attend the annual IMF Conference, he met with Kissinger and Scowcroft in New York (Source: Congressional Record, April 28, 1992).

Just months after resigning from Kissinger Associates to join the Bush Administration, Mr. Scowcroft was heavily involved in the handling of the BNL scandal, including winning approval of the $1 billion CCC program for Iraq in late 1989. Mr. Scowcroft was also directly involved in trying to win release of the second $500 million CCC installment for Iraq in March 1990 (Source: Congressional Record, April 28, 1992).

Holding positions of power such as Eagleburger and Scowcroft held during the Bush Administration, means just that, power. Power to control the focus of the Justice Department's inquiry, or more accurately, non-inquiry, into the BNL scandal.

First, Attorney General Richard Thornburgh, then, his replacement, Attorney General William Barr, stonewalled inquiries from several congressional committees and the press concerning the Justice Department's handling of the scandal. Finally, on October 16, 1992, Barr appointed retired Federal Judge Fred Lacy to conduct an investigation of limited scope of the Justice Department's handling of the scandal.

From the very beginning it was clear Judge Lacy was nothing more than a lackey. The investigation ignored several of the more important issues raised during the course of the congressional investigations of prewar Iraq policy. Barr's letter to Lacy outlining his responsibilities, totally ignored charges that the White House and Commerce Department altered export licensing information prior to providing information to Congress. Lacy failed to interview key witnesses such as former Export Administration Director Dennis Kloske, and key documents showing White House involvement, were not requested.

Moreover, Attorney General Barr only gave Lacy six weeks to complete his inquiry. But the real shot to the jaw to American Citizen's right to know what its government is involved in: An entire appendix of the Lacy Report, supposedly packed with evidence showing the Justice Department and CIA were vindicated of any wrongdoing in their handling of the BNL case, were stamped with highest security classification in the land.

Stamping "security classification" on government documents to keep them secret is now the form our government uses to keep the Amerikan Citizen from knowing, hence, making accountable, what government officials are doing. In one year alone, the Bush Administration classified 7,117,017 documents, that is 19,000 documents per day. Who are these guys!!!

The Bush Administration Cabinet was so steeped in conflict-of-interest rules for dealing with Iraq that President Bush had to waive conflict-of-interest laws for eleven Cabinet Officers and Cabinet-level officials, so they could participate in the formulation of the United States response to the Iraqi invasion of Kuwait in August of 1990 (Source: Internal State Department memo dated August 8, 1990). These waivers were withheld from the public for almost 18 months.

It had become so obvious that violations of government ethics had become "business as usual", the House Judiciary Committee on July 9, 1992, asked for Attorney General Barr to appoint an independent prosecutor to investigate, in the Committee's words: "serious allegations of possible violations of Federal criminal statutes by highranking officials of the Executive Branch. The potential criminal conduct in question relates to activities by both current and former officials to illegally assist the regime of Saddam Hussein prior to the August 1990, invasion of Kuwait, and to attempt to conceal information about potential criminal activity from Congress through the making of false statements, the non-production, falsification or alteration of official records and other documents, and through otherwise misleading and obstructing Congress in its investigation of such matters."

The July 9, 1992, letter to Attorney General Barr by members of the House Judiciary Committee asking for a special prosecutor states: "Finally, allegations of irregularities in the Department's handling of a host of investigations touching upon U.S. policy to Iraq must be considered carefully from the standpoint of the Ethics in Government Act (authorizing an Independent Counsel). Of most obvious concern is the Department's actions in the Banca del Lavoro (BNL) litigation---including the scope and timing of the indictment finally brought, the circumstances surrounding the appointment and recusal of the U.S. Attorney in the district in which the matter was handled, the possible political interference of high Executive Branch officials with the line attorneys handling the case, the possible delay or withholding of classified information from the Atlanta prosecutors, and the sudden and unexpected plea bargaining arrangement by the Department with defendant Christopher Drogoul---an arrangement which the presiding Federal District Judge severely and publicly critized as "MYSTERIOUS AND UNSEEMLY", and in his view, warranted the appointment of an Independent Counsel."

At this juncture, neither Attorney General Barr nor present Attorney General Janet Reno have appointed an Independent Counsel to answer the House Judiciary Committee's requests.

Why? I've shown that the raid on the Branch Davidians in Waco, Texas occurred less than 48 hours after the World Trade Center Bombing. The Trade Center bombing was in response to policies carried out by the Bush Administration toward Iraq. The BNL affair was the mirror to the world, showing the level top government officials in the U.S. (as well as Great Britain, Germany, and France) would stoop to, in attaining wealth and maintaining power.

On February 25, 1993, the day before the World Trade Center bombing, Henry Gonzalez, House Banking Committee Chairman, got up on the House floor and read into the Congressional Record, the diary of Paolo DeVito, head of BNL's Atlanta Group, a group set up to respond to fallout from the scandal. The DeVito diary indicates that former Attorney General Griffin Bell's law firm, King and Spaulding, was a key player in devising and executing BNL's strategy for dealing with the Atlanta scandal.

King and Spaulding also assigned Bill Hendricks to the BNL case, who just happened to be the former Chief of the Fraud Section at the Justice Department, the unit responsible for signing off on any BNL indictment. And the kicker: he had resigned his post at the Justice Department the same day BNL was raided by the FBI, August 1989 (Source: Congressional Record).

DeVito's diary shows BNL hired former Nixon Administration Attorney General and Secretary of State William Rodgers and his law firm of Rodgers and Wells. Also hired by BNL was public relations firm Sawyer-Miller.

Congressman Gonzalez was sending a copy of DeVito's diary to the Justice Department to see if Rodgers and Wells, King and Spaulding, Sawyer-Miller and some other firms retained by BNL had complied with the provisions of the Foreign Agents Registration Act.

This diary revealed a meeting on March 17, 1990, between Ms. Robin Ross, Chief-of-Staff of the Attorney General, Edward Dennis, Assistant Attorney General in charge of the Criminal Division (Note: Edward Dennis would later be asked to author a review of the stand-off at Waco titled, "Evaluation of the Handling of the Branch Davidian Stand-off in Waco, Texas"), and Italian Ambassador Petrignani. Ross told Petrignani "There will be no surprises" apparently referring to the planned plea bargain of fall guy Christopher Drogoul.

On February 24, 1993, Gonzalez wrote Acting Attorney General Stuart Gerson, requesting he review documents involving the above mentioned attorneys to see if the Foreign Agents Registration Act had been violated (Note: Gerson was in charge of the Waco stand-off until Reno took over March 12, 1993).

Congressman Gonzalez was simply fulfilling a promise he made on the House floor January

21, 1993,the first day the new Clinton Administration took power. His quote:

"It is unfortunate that the legacy of President Bush and his top advisors such as Richard Thornburgh, William Barr, James Baker, Brent Scowcroft, Lawrence Eagleburger, Boyden Gray, and Robert Gates will be clouded by their inability to understand and accept a basic principle of democracy---the right of the people to know the truth about government policy. In the case of Iraqgate, the President and his advisors chose to obstruct my inquiries rather than cooperate. They chose to obfuscate the truth rather than to illuminate the public so that we can learn from our mistakes. The President and his top advisors chose a similiar path in the Iran-Contra affair. The truth played second fiddle to saving political reputations.

I am not discouraged by the Bush Administration's obstruction. I will not give up. I will request all BNL and Iraq-related documents from the new Clinton Administration, including requests for documents from the White House, State Department, Justice Department, and the CIA. I perceive that President Clinton, Vice-President Gore and their top advisors have a better grasp of the principles of democracy and the Constitution than did the previous administration. I trust that they will be fully cooperative. After all, it is the people that deserve the truth."

The truth. In the area of politics, the "truth" is what you are able to convince others of when the truth is on your side. When it isn't on your side, smoke and mirrors can be more than an adequate substitute, if one has political clout.

Photo shows the severe damage from early morning fire at Pacific Justice Center in Redway.

Photo by Donald Sw

Structure that had housed the "Green Sweep" court records.

Postcard received by the author from David Thibodeau, one of the nine survivors of the April 19, 1994, fire never indicted. This card was mailed from Greece on October 20, 1994. A prettier view than a six-foot by ten-foot prison cell in Texas has to offer.

The helicopter crash sight.

David Thibodeau discussing issues at the Veterans Hall in Garberville, Ca.

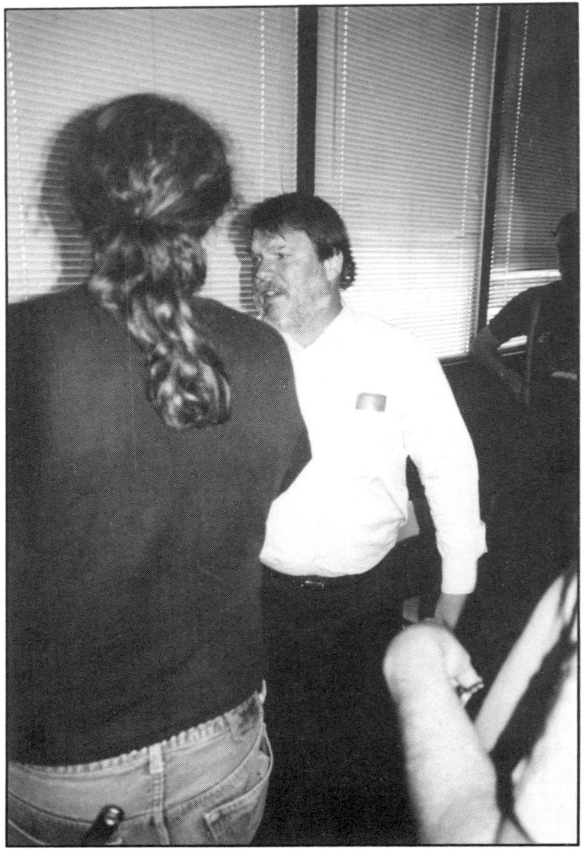

The author at the Veterans Hall meeting May 5, 1994.

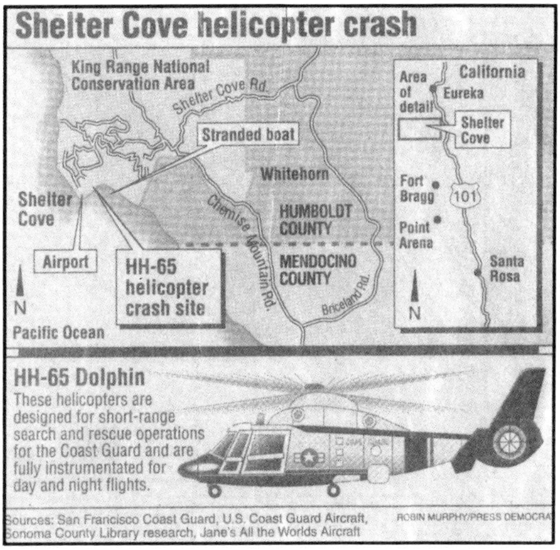

The FBI's "Moron of the Month" winner for the month of April, 1993. He remains nameless, which is as it should be.

Humboldt County Deputy Sheriff taking this author's low flight complaint, two months before the helicopter crashed, walking behind the tractor retrieving the pilot's body.

Lt. Laurence B. Williams

The young pilot of the craft. A friendlier, more courteous young man I have yet to meet. He possessed a degree in criminal justice.

The author's collie dog named "Charlie," sticking out his tongue after being told of Federal Judge Smith's ruling on Count Three at the Davidian trial in San Antonio.

November 23, 1994, Assistant Secretary of the Treasury for Enforcement Ronald Noble (second from left), giving the evil eye to the man in charge of the forces overseeing the recent shootout in Washington D.C. where two FBI agents were slain.

The Pontiff immediately after learning the author had just finished writing a book about Waco and the Branch Davidians!!!

MAIL OUT REPORT

HUMBOLDT COUNTY SHERIFF'S DEPARTMENT
826 Fourth Street
Eureka, CA 95501

SHERIFF'S OFFICE USE ONLY		Report No.
[ ] Felony	[ ] Infraction	94-2589
[X] Misdemeanor	[ ] Incident	Area
Section/Code/Description 602(m) P.C. TRESSPASS		32

Instructions:
1. Type or print in ball point pen only.
2. Be as descriptive as possible in identifying persons and property.
3. Use additional pages if necessary to complete the report.
4. Return the completed report in the envelope provided within 30 days.
5. The report is an official record to be used for investigative purposes.

Reporting Party (Name and address):
Ronald Davidson
Box 301
Miranda, Ca. 95553

Location of incident (Address or describe): River Rd. & PhillipsvilleRd.

Type of location (Home, business, etc.): Home

Day of incident — Mo/day/yr: 5/7/94 — Time: 1:50&2:10 p.m.

Method, device, tool, or instrument used: helicopter

VICTIM: (Last)	(First)	(Middle)	Race	Sex	Birthdate	Age
Davidson	Ronald	Ray	white	male	6/11/47	46

Address: [x] Residence [ ] Business — Box 301 — City: Miranda — State: Ca. — Zip: 95553 — Phone: 943-3119

OTHER: (Last)	(First)	(Middle)	Race	Sex	Birthdate	Age
Lai	Sue	Ching	chinese/ American	female	12/15/58	36

Address: [x] Residence [ ] Business — same — City — State — Zip — Phone: 943-3119

Vehicles involved (Year, make, model, color, license number, state, any damage, etc.)
orange helicopter

Give a brief description of the incident:
Helicopter flew over my house at high rate of speed, twice, within 20 minutes, under 200 feet. Was dangerous, uncalled for, low altitude, trespass. I called Coast Guard and pilot Larry Williams, returned my call and admitted he was the pilot that had flown over. First claimed height of 850 ft. I disputed this height and while he was recording the talk, seemed to change his stance, somewhat, as to the height. As I watched him turn west, he was so low he had to gain altitude to miss the tree tops on a ridge west of 101, ridge approx. 300 ftelev.

Fully describe what was [ ] Stolen [ ] Lost [ ] Damaged	Serial No.	$$$Value
1.		
2.		
3.		
4.		

I declare under penalty of perjury that the foregoing report is true and correct.

Ronald R Davidson
Your signature

SHERIFF'S OFFICE USE ONLY
[ ] Further Investigation [ ] File, No Further Investigation [ ] No Crime

Reviewed by ______ Date ______

HCSD 0631.7 Rev 11/92

MAIL OUT REPORT

HUMBOLDT COUNTY SHERIFF'S DEPARTMENT
826 Fourth Street
Eureka, CA 95501

SHERIFF'S OFFICE USE ONLY		Report No.
[ ] Felony	[ ] Infraction	94-8707
[ ] Misdemeanor	[X] Incident	Area
Section/Code/Description: COAST GUARD OVER FLIGHTS		32

Instructions:
1. Type or print in ball point pen only.
2. Be as descriptive as possible in identifying persons and property.
3. Use additional pages if necessary to complete the report.
4. Return the completed report in the envelope provided within 30 days.
5. The report is an official record to be used for investigative purposes.

Reporting Party (Name and address):

Location of incident (Address or describe): CORNER OF Phillipsville RD & RIVER RD. in Phillipsville

Type of location (Home, business, etc.): Home

Day of incident: 12/18/94 Mo/day/yr Time 3:30 am (pm)

Method, device, tool, or instrument used: Helicopter

VICTIM: (Last)	(First)	(Middle)	Race	Sex	Birthdate	Age
DAVIDSON	RONALD	RAY	White	Male	6-11-47	47

Address:	[X] Residence	[ ] Business	City	State	Zip	Phone
Box 301			MIRANDA,	CA	95553	943-3119

OTHER: (Last)	(First)	(Middle)	Race	Sex	Birthdate	Age
—						

Address:	[ ] Residence	[ ] Business	City	State	Zip	Phone

Vehicles involved (Year, make, model, color, license number, state, any damage, etc.)
COAST GUARD Helicopter

Give a brief description of the incident:
Helicopter FLEW OVER my place at 60 mph. APPROX., Banked to the Left, then made A LEFT turn at tree top level and FLEW toward the coast (west). APPROX. one hour Later, pilot SAID his "mission" WAS to FLY at 350'. I have pilot admitting he WAS UNDER 500 Ft Level. This is 3RD time since may

Fully describe what was [ ] Stolen [ ] Lost [ ] Damaged	Serial No.	$$$Value
1.		
2.		
3.		
4.		

I declare under penalty of perjury that the foregoing report is true and correct.

Ronald R Davidson
Your signature

SHERIFF'S OFFICE USE ONLY
[ ] Further [ ] File, No Further Investigation [ ] No Crime

[signature] Lt.
Reviewed by

12-19-94
Date

HCSD 0631.7 Rev 11/92

After Bill Clinton took power in January of 1993, he appointed Senator Lloyd Bentsen of Texas as Treasury Secretary. And Clinton appointed Roger Altman as Deputy Secretary, second only to Bentsen in the Treasury Department hierarchy.

Altman was a high school classmate of Bill Clinton's while they were growing up in Arkansas.

After delving into the Congressional Directory 1993-1994, we discover both Lloyd Bentsen and Roger Altman sit on the Resolution Trust Corporation and the Thrift Depositor Oversight Protection Board. These "independent agencies" were created on August 9, 1989, to oversee and investigate our nation's failed Savings and Loans.

According to the General Accounting Office, 57 per cent of all losses from the criminal fraud perpetrated by insiders of Savings and Loans occurred in Texas.

Failed Texas institutions account for 41 percent of the federal money spent on the S&L bailout. The Texas thrifts' raid on the public treasury will cost every Amerikan $2,200.

The Resolution Trust Corporation has spent five years and tens of millions of dollars investigating the collapse of Texas S&L's. It has accomplished very little.

It has recovered fewer than $19 million in settlements from insiders who were running the thrifts. Not one RTC liability case has ever reached a jury in Texas. NOT ONE.

Congress explicitly gave the agency subpoena power in 1990, so that it could follow the money trail (Note: fat-ass Buck Revell's Dallas office allegedly gives top priority to bank and savings and loan fraud. Source: "The FBI, by Ronald Kessler).

In defending their use of subpoenas against a legal challenge in 1993, RTC lawyers told the District of Columbia Court of Appeals that subpoena power was essential to understanding the personal financial dealings between S&L insiders and borrowers---including bribes and kickbacks---because such information isn't usually available in S&L records.

Yet the agency did not issue even a single subpoena in its investigation of 86 of 137 failed Texas S&L's. The entire Houston office of the RTC issued only three subpoenas in its investigation of 37 failed S&L's (Source: Thomas J. Burnside, senior lawyer with RTC from 1990-1993, New York Times, May 1994).

By contrast, the Whitewater special prosecutor, Robert Fiske, issued 160 grand jury subpoenas to investigate tiny Madison Guaranty.

The feeble investigation of the collapse in Texas is generally attributed to "operational problems" or bureaucratic turf battles. The RTC has gone through several crippling reorganizations in recent years.

No lawyer who recommended a suit against a Texas S&L insider or professional before 1993, is still handling the case today.

The RTC's failures were too purposeful to be to be just gross incompetence. Anytime a high-profile lawsuit is brought against a powerful figure, it is politically risky and expensive. The agency's leadership set up a system to avoid that risk.

The incentive was for lawyers to perform a listless overview of bank records rather than vigorously investigate wrongdoers. And there was hardly any political pressure for things to change.

Democrats and Republicans alike have had little desire for public scrutiny of the gory aftermath of their legislative and regulatory largesse to S&L's.

The RTC's lapses became most pronounced when Roger Altman ran the agency from April 1993 until March 1994 (Writer's note: Altman began running the RTC the same month the Mt. Carmel Center was torched).

Within a month of taking control, he reversed the RTC's longstanding request to Congress to extend the Federal statute of limitations on investigating S&L wrongdoing.

Altman later commissioned a task force that, in a report to Congress, defended the RTC investigation in Texas and belittled the cost of Texas thrifts to taxpayers.

A former Chief RTC investigator in Texas told Congress in May of 1994, that this was "a whitewash of a national scandal" (Source: Thomas J. Burnside, senior lawyer with RTC from 1990-1993, New York Times, May 1994).

Altman departed the Treasury Department in August of 1994, brought down with the help of the diary his special assistant, Joshua Steiner, revealed to the Senate Banking Committee during their hearings on the Whitewater affair.

This is the same guy that alerted Altman about the raid to take place on the Branch

Davidians, assuming Altman didn't already know (Source: Treasury Department Report on Waco, page 178), and Altman did nothing.

The House Banking Committee also had hearings on the Whitewater affair, headed by none other than Henry Gonzalez of Texas. Remember Henry, the man that said the Amerikan people deserved the truth about the BNL scandal. The man whose offices in Texas were located less than one block from the Federal Court where 11 Branch Davidian victims were railroaded into prison. Victims, because mirrors and lights were needed to blind the Amerikan public to the raw truth.

When we cover the mirrors and dim the lights, what do we have? Well, we have a Treasury Secretary in charge of the two independent agencies authorized to oversee the S&L debauchery, coming from a state more culpable than any other, by far. We have a Deputy Secretary on those same boards whose high school buddy is now the President, and is in need of having his backside covered because of his own indiscretions while Governor of Arkansas, and we have a number of former Bush Administration official assholes wondering if a new Attorney General will follow Henry Gonzalez' request, and use a microscope on them rather than a mirror.

The answer for those culpable individuals is obvious: get the Justice Department behind the eight ball. Less than six weeks after taking office, Janet Reno had given the order to execute what became the largest single disaster in law enforcement history in the U.S., by far. She said she would resign if asked to do so. Only Congressman John Conyers of Michigan, had the integrity to demand her resignation.

Why no Republicans asked should be obvious. Only a handful asking and Reno would have been gone. No, now they had her on a string.

And as the Congressional Directory 1993-1994 illustrates, vacancies in the Justice Department's key positions remained the rule rather than the exception.

How was this cooption accomplished? We need to look at the stand-off, the 51 days of total government control to see if we can glean, as outsiders looking in from a distance, what our government was seeking to accomplish, when the Treasury Department gave the green light and attempted to execute the largest law enforcement action on Citizens in United States history, in the middle of Nowhere, Texas.

THE STAND-OFF---RECIPE FOR FAILURE

On the evening of the failed raid, the Treasury Department asked for assistance from the FBI. The FBI agreed to render use of the Hostage Rescue Team (the team that fat-ass Revell created), on condition that the Treasury Department give <u>full</u> control to the Justice Department. Treasury agreed to do so.

Following the inauguration of President Clinton, the Justice Department was in a care-taker mode, with senior career officials running the day-to-day affairs of the department, with Bush Administration official holdover Stuart Gerson performing the function of Attorney General.

A White House laison team, led by Webster Hubbell (Writer's note: Hubbell has since resigned as a result of the Whitewater affair), would report to Gerson and Gerson, in turn, would report to the White House.

The Criminal Division was under the direction of Deputy Assistant Attorney General John C. Keeney, when the stand-off began. No Senate-confirmed appointees of President Clinton had yet arrived at the Justice Department (Source: The Treasury Department Report on Waco).

Once the FBI notified Gerson that the FBI would be taking over the negotiations in Waco, they also notified, on the same day, James S. Reynolds, Chief of the Criminal Division's Terrorism and Violent Crimes Section. The next day Reynolds assigned Mary Incontro, his Deputy Chief For Violent Crime, to keep track of, and to apprise Reynolds of all developments regarding both the stand-off and investigation/prosecution of the Davidians.

If there were any connections between the World Trade Center bombing and the raid on Waco Davidians, James S. Reynolds would be overseeing both situations. Remember, his man in New York, James Fox, was only two blocks from the Trade Center when it exploded (Fox would be relieved of his duties in December of 1993 for talking to the press).

Soon after the stand-off began, the FBI requested Gerson approve the use of military vehicles to assist them in "limited tactical maneuvers" to secure and tighten the perimeter around Mt. Carmel. Gerson gave the o.k. and called White House Chief of Staff Thomas McLarty (since resigned over the Whitewater affair) to notify him of the change.

Moments later President Clinton called Gerson back, wanting to know why military vehicles were being deployed, since Clinton had been promised by the FBI and Gerson that the approach to resolving the crisis would be "negotiate, watch, and contain."

Apparently, Gerson satisfied the President's curiosity, and promised to keep Clinton informed if the FBI were to adopt more aggressive tactics.

On March 8, 1993, Gerson discovered that FBI Director William Sessions wanted to go to Waco to negotiate directly with Koresh. Sessions felt that, since he was a former U.S. Attorney and U.S. District Judge from the Western District of Texas, and since he once lived in Waco, he would have credibility with those inside Mt. Carmel. Needless to say, Gerson told the man in charge of the crisis, he could not run the crisis as as he deemed necessary.

Within months Sessions would be removed as FBI Director. Congressman Gonzalez, in praising Sessions for his cooperation with the House Banking Committee during the Commitee's investigation of the BNL scandal, said Sessions was a man of great integrity (probably why he was pushed aside) and Gonzalez hoped Sessions would fight the attempt to have him removed from the Directorship. Was Sessions removal related to his behind the scenes actions in trying to resolve the stand-off?

Four days after Sessions attempt to go to Waco, Gerson decided it was time to turn the reins over to Webster Hubbell. On March 12, 1993, Janet Reno was confirmed by the Senate and took over as Attorney General. Gerson didn't brief her about events that had transpired since he had been in charge of the situation (Source: The Treasury Department Report On Waco). Why? Its clear now that Reno needed all the help she could get. The FBI briefed Reno.

From the time the stand-off began on February 28, 1993, the main actors in Washington D.C. responsible for planning and decision-making, rested with the Terrorism and Violent Crimes Section of the Justice Department's Criminal Division (TVCS/CRM) and the Violent Crimes and Major Offenders Section (VCMOS) of the FBI's Criminal Investigation Division (CID).

As Chief of the TVCS/CRM, James Reynolds called the shots and had the backing of Deputy Chief Incontro and section attorney John Lancaster. Deputy Attorney General Mark Richard oversaw the activities of TVCS/CRM. And the everpresent kicker: Richard was one of the Justice Department attorneys that met with Italian Ambassador Petrignani to assure him that there would "not be any surprises" referring to the bank fraud indictment and future plea bargain of BNL Atlanta bank manager Christopher Drogoul (remember one other participant in this meeting was Edward Dennis, writer of the Justice Department evaluation of the Justice Department handling of Waco).

Attorney General Reno would be dependent on Richard in the latter stages of the standoff to keep her informed and "help" advise her of her options (Source: Attorney General Report On Waco).

The primary role of Reynolds as TVCS Chief was to keep the peace between the U.S. Attorney's office (USAO) for the Western District of Texas and the VCMOS at FBI headquarters.

This precarious peace ended March 23, 1993, when Bill Johnston (remember him, he brought reporters for the Waco-Herald Tribune and ATF together in his Waco office prior to the raid and refused to sign the search warrant if a siege approach was adopted rather than dynamic entry) wrote a letter to Attorney General Reno, complaining about decisions being made affecting the investigation of the shootings of the ATF agents, made by then U.S. Attorney Ronald Ederer.

Apparently, Ederer instructed Johnston to refrain from assembling an investigative team consisting of Texas Rangers, other agencies and crime laboratories to work on the homicide case. And Ederer didn't want Johnston to accept an offer of assistance from a local District Attorney's office. Inquiries by those outside the Federal domain must be strictly controlled.

Johnston also was concerned about possible destruction of evidence by the FBI using tanks to push vehicles away from the Mt. Carmel Center. The ATF used these vehicles for cover during the shoot-out and trajectory evidence was being destroyed.

Or were the tanks removing them to hide what really occurred during the raid? The films of the actual raid show the ATF shooting into the Center, but fail to show any vehicles being hit by return fire.

In discussions with James Reynolds and Robert McNamara, the Assistant General Counsel For Enforcement at the Treasury Department between March 26-29, Deputy Assistant Attorney General Richard learned there was mutiny abrewin' among the various agencies involved in the investigation. Richard also learned about his boss, Janet Reno, requesting a review be made of the entire situation in Waco.

Richard also discovered that Reno or Special Assistant Attorney General Webb Hubbell (since resigned as a result of the Whitewater affair) had been contacted by a Congressman over the issue of FBI destruction of evidence (Source: Attorney General Report on Waco).

Sensing that spin doctors can't control a mutiny, Richard proposed removing the case from San Antonio and having a team of Assistant U.S. Attorneys report directly to the Criminal Division in, where else, Washington D.C. On April 7, 1993, Richard and Reynolds traveled to Waco to redefine the roles of the various parties to the action.

Richard met privately with Johnston. He got Johnston to agree to the changes. Johnston's reward was to be a member of the courtroom prosecution team. What an honor!! The roles of the FBI and the Texas Rangers, basically remained the same. Now, all parties were to funnel results of their investigations through Washington, D.C., under doctors orders.

Richard claimed this April 7, 1993, trip to Waco allowed him the first opportunity to learn about the FBI's proposed use of gas on the Mt. Carmel Center to end the stand-off. Deputy Director Clarke and Associate Deputy Director Potts of the FBI, were in Waco during this time and discussed in detail, the use of CS gas to end the impass (Source: The Attorney General Report on Waco).

At a meeting the week of April 12, 1993, at the White House, in the office of White House Counsel Bernard Nussbaum, Webster Hubbell explained that the FBI would have to pull the HRT back for training exercises if the stand-off continued indefinitely. He also cited lack of any progress.

Hubbell's reasoning is sound, if the listener suffers from a shortage of brain cells. After all, the function of training exercises is to prepare one for a stand-off. Impatience with lack of progress is in conflict with the "negotiate, watch, and contain" approach the FBI, and Gerson, promised Clinton when they requested military tanks early on in the stand-off.

The truth is, during the 51 day stand-off, over 700 law enforcement personnel participated in the effort to end the stand-off. Between 250-300 FBI personnel were present in Waco at any given time, along with hundreds of officers and agents from other federal, state, and local agencies (Source: The Attorney General Report on Waco).

The truth is that the need for a diversion to take the heat off "The Big Apple" had been accomplished. The suspects allegedly responsible for the World Trade Center bombing, had either fled the country or were behind bars.

As discussed earlier, Dan Rather of CBS News, revealed in reports broadcast in July 1993, that the FBI had been monitoring the meetings between the planners of the bombing through an informant, wired for sound. This informant, according to the FBI in Rather's news story, to gain credibility with the other planners, WAS THE ACTUAL SUPPLIER OF THE DETONATING DEVICE.

This means the FBI knew BEFOREHAND, who was involved in the bombing. It also contradicts the statement fat-ass Buck Revell made on "60 Minutes" November 13, 1994, stating the FBI had a notebook of El Sayyid Nosair, detailing plans to commit terrorist acts that included bombing the World Trade Center, but never read it. Never read it. They think we're morons!!!

The diversion to Waco, less than 48 hours after the Trade Center bombing, was necessary to take the extreme heat off government officials trying to cope with the accompanying fall-out and public paranoia the bombing generated.

After 30 days of the Waco stand-off, with

the alleged perpetrators of the Trade Center bombing jailed, city life was back to normal. Letterman was slipping us David Koresh jokes by night and Regis and Kathy selling us "Fun-ship Carnival" cruises by day.

Mt. Carmel and its band of polygamist/celibate, machine-gun marauding, child molesting, shit-in-a-bucket, vegetarian yogurt eating, wacky Waco hillbilly Christians, whose messianic leader was a rockstar wannabe named "Howell" (pronounced howl), had become expendable. A thorn in the side of the new administration. Who knows, Koresh's womanizing skills may have generated a bit of envy from President Bubba.

Hindsight is always 20/20. We all have now learned enough about Whitewater to recognize that key members of the Clinton team, as well as key members of the former Bush Administration (i.e. Edward Dennis and Mark Richard proclivities to plea bargain the farm away), could sleep easier if they had the most powerful prosecutor in Amerika on a leash of proper length.

The meeting mentioned above in Nussbaum's office during the week of April 12, 1993, may have been when "the team" formulated its strategy. Whatever was hashed out remains hazy because those participating couldn't, or wouldn't, remember the date of the meeting. Participants included Nussbaum, Hubbell, Senior Advisor Bruce Lindsay, and now deceased White House Deputy Counsel Vince Foster (Source: The Attorney General Report on Waco).

There has been much speculation concerning the death of Foster. Most speculate his death is connected to the inside knowledge he posessed dealing with the Whitewater affair. The claim that Nussbaum went to Foster's office and removed files related to Whitewater, fuels this line of speculation. The video-cassette circulating the country titled, "The Clinton Chronicles" desires, I believe, to take our minds away from the truth surrounding the Waco tragedy. The road to hell is paved with good intentions.

Clearly, Foster's death was something other than suicide. The number of factual inconsistencies with death by suicide continue to baffle even the most astute spin doctors.

For instance, the gun used is not in the victim's hand after a self-inflicted head wound, but Foster died with the gun still in his hand. Normally, the gun has blood on it, not Foster's. Also, initial reports stated there were no powder burns on Foster's hands or face. The gun used was a 1911 or 1913 Colt 38. It had no serial numbers and was untraceable. Foster's family had never seen it previously. The alleged suicide note turned up in Foster's briefcase five days after it had been searched by a Park Police officer, who found nothing useful inside the briefcase during the initial search. A housing development and a manned construction site were only about 100 yards from where the shot was fired. No one reported hearing a gunshot.

If those facts don't raise your eyebrows, Park Police and the White House responses won't help. The Wall Street Journal has sued Park Police for not turning over the autopsy and information about the crime scene in accordance with the Freedom of Information Act. They think we're morons!!!

When Foster's office was searched by the

Park Police, they didn't find a desk calendar or appointment book. The White House isn't releasing Foster's phone logs.

President Clinton admits talking to Foster for a half-hour the night before his death.

Did Nussbaum, Hubbell, Lindsay, and Foster possess knowledge of a more sinister FBI tactical plan that went far beyond mere use of CS gas? Did Foster's conscience, after months of trying to reconcile being party to a decision that ultimately resulted in the deaths of over 80 people, including 17 children under the age of 10, finally get to Foster ?

After the meeting mentioned above with Hubbell, Nussbaum told the President that the handling of the stand-off was "a Department of Justice call, not a White House call" (Source: The Attorney General Report on Waco). This approach would effectively place accountability for any failures on the Attorney General.

But was it really Reno's call? On April 16, 1993, three days before the Waco barbeque, Richard met with Hubbell and Carl Stern, Director of the Office of Public Affairs (a fancy title for what is, essentially, the resident spin doctor). According to Richard, Hubbell advised him that the Attorney General had disapproved the plan using CS gas to end the stand-off. Hubbell then asked Richard what he thought the FBI's reaction might be. Richard answered that the FBI wouldn't be pleased, that they would, nonetheless, accept the decision, and that they may then talk of withdrawal.

Withdrawal? Withdrawal? After four federal agents were killed and 16 wounded? Withdrawal? And if the FBI withdrew, who would take the heat? Reno really had no choice.

She was far out of her league, anyway. A chemistry major in college, past 50 and never married, physically built more like a man than a woman, a more graceless creature meandering through the halls of Justice Department drones at work, I can't imagine. Her form of devolution with respect to social I.Q., was the perfect match if placing the power of the Attorney General's office on hold was the goal.

Now Reno finds herself matching wits with the current and former Commanders of the Delta Force, the military elite. The "Don't ask, don't tell" policy wasn't in effect when Reno met with these Commanders on April 14, 1993, to discuss the gassing of the Davidians. But I can imagine the snickers and toilet jokes exchanged once the meeting broke up.

Reno had to be leary of the precarious position she occupied. At the April 16, 1993, meeting between Richard, Hubbell, and Stern, Stern commented that going ahead with the plan might be looked down on by the public, and likened it to the gassing of the Kurds by Saddam Hussein (Source: The Attorney General Report on Waco).

To cover her tracks, Reno, on April 16, requested the preparation of a documented statement describing the situation inside the Mt. Carmel Center, the progress of the negotiations,and the merits of the proposal. The Terrorism and violent Crimes Deputy Chief Mary Incontro, wrote up the document.

The document was clearly nothing more than

an attempt by Reno to cover her own broad ass. Reno didn't read the prepared statement carefully, nor did she read the supporting documentation provided along with the statement (Source: The Attorney General Report on Waco).

Now the results of Reno's decision to allow the gassing of the residents of Mt. Carmel is history, or in this case, herstory. I'm not privy to conversations between those holding positions of power when decisions to act are made. Few of us are. But we can see the harvest reaped by decisions made through those in positions of power.

Earlier, I stated evidence that pointed to connections between the World Trade Center bombing and the raid on the Mt. Carmel Center. Both events were investigated by the FBI's Terrorism and Violent Crimes Section, headed by James S. Reynolds.

Henry Gonzalez, Chairman of the House Banking Committee, named numerous members of the Bush Administration as having been neck deep in the unlawful acts related to the Iraqi military buildup that preceded Desert Storm.

Among those named were members of the National Security Council, including former President Bush and Brent Scowcroft. Reynolds, as Chief of the FBI's Terrorism and Violent Crimes Section, is the FBI's laison to the National Security Council. Get it??

According to the CBS News reports aired in July 1993, the FBI had an informant acting as a co-conspirator in the bombing plot. Bilal Alkaisi, 28, of Palestinian descent, was arrested and indicted in the conspiracy, but his case was severed from the four men convicted in the bombing, and his lawyer said he was hoping to settle the case without a trial (Source: Richard Bernstein, New York Times, March 5, 1994).

The two Iraqis that allegedly built the bomb, Ramzi Yousef and Abdul Rahman Yasin, were said to have fled the U.S. for Iraq immediately after the bombing (Source: Richard Bernstein).

What benefits accrued (whether by design or happenstance) to the former Bush Administration officials looking over their shoulder after Congressman Gonzalez informed them via his speech delivered on the House floor January 21, 1993, of Gonzalez' intent to carry on with the BNL investigation?

One thing the bombing did was generate widespread fear of Islamic fundamentalists within our large metropolitan areas, thus placing more sentiment by the public toward a crackdown on suspected Islamic terrorists.

Within months of the Trade Center bombing, more arrests were made and trial dates set for more than a dozen people, including a blind Muslim Cleric, on charges that they were part of a broad conspiracy to blow up New York City landmarks and assassinate political leaders.

With that type of action going on in legal circles, Bush was being held in higher esteem than ever for his actions toward Iraq. Gonzalez would be hard pressed to get support for his investigation now.

The bombing also allowed top Treasury Department officials to support a coordinated effort to divert the public's attention away from events of the moment in the interest of calming public fear and paranoia, and posible backlashes against those in the Arab communities.

Could the timing of the events been even more sinister than any of us want to believe? Could Treasury have been a willing partner as part of a trade-off? Remember, Treasury Secretary Lloyd Bentsen (conveniently out of the U.S. at the time of the raid on Mt. Carmel) had given up his U.S. Senate seat from Texas. Discussed earlier was the sordid fact that Texas accounts for 61% of the monetary losses nationwide, from the failed Savings and Loan debauchery.

And the second in command at Treasury, and in charge of the Resolution Trust Corporation oversight of S&L fraud, Roger Altman, was a high school classmate and confident of President Clinton's at the time of the Mt. Carmel raid. In fact, Altman lost his position at Treasury for failing to testify to Congress in a forthright manner concerning his contacts with members of the Executive Branch relating to Clinton's involvement with a failed Savings and Loan in Arkansas while Clinton was Governor. In essence, Altman was forced to abdicate his position in treasury by compromising the credibility his high governmental position required.

The Treasury Department Report On Waco reveals that Joshua Steiner, Altman's then Special Assistant, alerted Altman to the raid plan. Steiner was a key player in bringing Altman to resign, by revealing incriminating excerpts Steiner had written in his diary. What does his diary reveal concerning Altman's state of mind with regard to actions taken by Treasury involving the raid on the Branch Davidians at Mt. Carmel?

It was just hours after the World Trade Center bombing that then Acting Deputy Assistant Secretary For Law Enforcement (overseer of ATF) Michael D. Langan was made aware of the proposed raid by a memorandum prepared just MINUTES after the World Trade Center bombing by Christopher Cuyler, ATF's laison to the Treasury Department.

Red flags must have appeared before Langan's eyes. He responded by calling a conference that included John P. Simpson, Acting Assistant Secretary For Enforcement, Stanley Morris, former Director of the U.S. Marshal's Service (now working in the Office of Enforcement), and Ronald K. Noble, Clinton's designee as Secretary for Law Enforcement in the Treasury Department (Source: Treasury Department Report On Waco, pages 177, 178).

They all agreed the raid required excessive force to execute the warrant, precautions to protect both ATF agents and Davidians were absent, and chances of achieving the mission's goal without a shoot-out were slim. Therefore, Simpson called ATF Director Higgins and directed that the raid be called off (Source: The Treasury Department Report On Waco, page 179).

Less than an hour later (if you believe the Treasury Department Report On Waco) Higgins called Simpson back and in a three-way conversation that included Noble, got them to revoke their order that had, just minutes before, concluded the raid plan was fraught with potential catastrophies that, less than 44 hours later, evolved from potential, to ACTUAL CATASTROPHIES, including deaths of both agents and Davidians.

What occurred during such a small window of time to motivate Noble and Simpson to claim they revoked the order calling off the raid?

The bombing, which occurred at 12:18 p.m. on February 26, 1993, just hours before Simpson's revoking order, heavily damaged Secret Service and Customs facilities, raising concerns within the Office of Enforcement over possible injuries to Secret Service and Customs Personnel (agencies under the purview of Noble and Simpson). ATF personnel were already playing a major role in the investigation of the bombing.

Would prudent career civil servants, attempting to deal with the massive disaster that had just vibrated their consciousness, and would demand their total, complete, and undivided attention, now revoke an order that would allow its understudy to engage in the largest law enforcement action in U.S. history? And become the largest disaster in civilian law enforcement history!!!!!

Who did Higgins communicate with upon completion of his first conversation with Simpson? If Secretary Bentsen was out of the country or incommunicado (a doubtful proposition in light of the Trade Center bombing), the only Treasury official with the authority to overrule Simpson was Roger Altman.

Where's Steiner's diary? Why isn't it forthcoming? Why have no government officials taking part in the House Appropriations Committee hearings looked at the STARK NAKEDNESS the Treasury Department is left with upon closer scrutiny of the events occurring in New York on February 26, 1993, and those occurring in Nowhere, Texas, less than two days later, involving the same agency? Why???

The Treasury Department Report On Waco admits its "independent" inquiry adopted a "don't ask, don't tell" policy with regard to interviewing those members of Congress attending the CLOSED Special Executive Session of the Subcommittee Hearings held March 10, 1993, in the beginning stages of the 51 day stand-off. And the Report made only limited inquiries of others who possessed knowledge about what was discussed during the session.

What the hell is going on here??? There is a dead skunk in the middle of the road, stinking to high heaven.

We've seen that the man holding the position of Director of the FBI, William Sessions, wasn't even allowed to visit Waco during the stand-off. Did Director Sessions see the connection between the World Trade Center bombing (possibly knowing it was Iraqi retaliation for Desert Storm), and the timing of the raid on Mt. Carmel?

During the height of the presidential campaign, on October 11, 1992, Sam Donaldson, newscaster for ABC Primetime, revealed the Justice Department was investigating possible indiscretions by Sessions related to his actions in carrying out his duties as Director.

Donaldson also cited opposing sources that said this investigation came about because the Justice Department, and Attorney General William Barr, feared the FBI was about to reveal the truth about the Bush Administration's cover-up of its illegal financing and profiteering from its clandestine Iraqi foreign policy (Source: The FBI, by Ronald Kessler, page 408).

House Banking Committee Chairman Henry Gonzalez revealed that Director Sessions stood alone in the Justice Department, in refusing to assist in the Justice Department cover-up of the BNL criminal conspiracy (Source: Congressional Record, January 25, 1993).

Curiously, the Clinton campaign team failed to exploit this potential bombshell, at the critical stage of the presidential campaign. Why???

It is as if those in power positions with authority to seek the truth concerning the World Trade Center bombing and its related Waco raid, are under a spell. Or maybe they fear getting the Vince Foster remedy.

If Vince Foster's death was a suicide, no student of the law would seriously suggest an intelligent, experienced lawyer, schooled in the art of persuasion and who spent his life fixing other people's problems, would kill himself when the competition got tough. Circumstances surrounding Whitewater and the lawyering skills it required, is what a guy like Vince Foster is all about.

But dealing with one's conscience while the blood of 90 victims calls from the ground for justice, competing with one's conscience over issues like that, is what suicide is all about.

But if Foster's death was intentional murder, what preceded his death that necessitated his elimination? Was Foster considering going public with insider knowledge he possessed, that would incriminate high government officials, both past and present, who were involved in the Trade Center bombing and Waco raid?

These two events were the only ones of substance during Foster's short tenure as Deputy White House Counsel. The Whitewater affair only gained momentum and publicity, many months after Foster's death.

Much of what I've discussed above, that points to a connection between the BNL scandal, the World Trade Center bombing, and the Waco raid, was extracted from the so-called "independent" government investigations commissioned by the Treasury Department and the Justice Department. Surprisingly, no connection was made by those agencies. Why???

What other credible sources can be drawn on to buttress the argument that our government's credibility is bankrupt with regard to its official version of what occurred on February 26, 1993, and what truly motivated the raid on Mt. Carmel two days later?

TRIED BY FIRE, SEX, LIES

BUT NOT VIDEOTAPE

The morning of April 19, 1993, I turned on my television and satellite receiver, and began looking for the feed from the Waco Convention Center. I was hungry for my daily dose of jeopardy, Washington D.C.'s ATF/FBI version of the daily double. We all know the rules, if you lie and lose, you lose twice the bet.

What I found was a transponder with the camera focused on the Mt. Carmel Center. Tanks were systematically tearing holes in specific areas, and those in charge claimed CS gas was being inserted. We would later learn that CS gas is highly flammable. The weather forecast predicted a windy day in the area of Mt. Carmel, winds to peak around noon, at approximately 30 miles per hour.

By now media personnel and equipment had been moved further back from the action, over 3-1/2 miles from the scene. Fire trucks that had been on the scene, had been driven back to their local fire departments, under orders to return when called back, if needed.

Evidence received through discovery requests by attorneys presently suing the Federal government over the Waco assault, show extensive amounts of a cyanide compound was found in most of the deceased Davidians during postmortem exams.

Documents from Aldrich Chemical, the makers of CS gas, report that the chemical compound is a high-temperature incendiary and should not be used in enclosed buildings.

Further, CS is a chlorinated nitrile cyclic hydrocarbon which produces cyanide gas when burned at high temperature. Documents provided by Aldrich, state that water should not be used to extinguish burning CS because there is a danger of generating a hydrogen cyanide (HCN) cloud.

HCN is an extremely lethal toxic gas used by the military as a chemical weapon (Blood Agent AC), and by penal institutions to execute prisoners. It is also the active ingredient in Zyklon B, the agent alleged to have been used by the Nazis to execute Jews.

Media video footage shows several federal agents (or Delta Forces) dressed in black and wearing a Scott breathing apparatus outside the burning structure of Mt. Carmel. Recall that the FBI didn't call the fire department when the fire started, and held back the fire engines when they finally did arrive, until the fire was nearly out.

I don't need an olfactometer to tell me there is another dead skunk in the middle of the road!!

As I continued watching the tanks crush Mt. Carmel, a plume of smoke appeared in a corner of the building, followed by flames, just as a tank exited that spot. If the Feds were intent on torching the place, the location and timing of the fire (with respect to peaking winds and media vantage point), was a professional job.

The fire that consumed Mt. Carmel was the most intense I've ever witnessed. The fact that it was fueled by high winds, and the holes opened by the tanks acted like opening a flue in a wood stove, still doesn't account for the intensity of heat I witnessed.

In addition, the black smoke that continued to bellow from the flames, far exceeded what would be expected from a few cans of Coleman lantern fuel the Davidians allegedly used to start the fire.

Who started the fire? Does it really matter? At the trial of the Davidians in San Antonio, the government produced tapes they claim had voices from inside Mt. Carmel saying, "Light the fire." A sniper claims to have seen a man cup his hands, as one would do to light a match in the wind, and flames erupting shortly thereafter.

The prosecution claims the government had a plane with heat-sensing equipment flying overhead at precisely the same time of the fire, and that this plane photographed the scene. They claim the photos show fires beginning in at least four separate locations simultaneously.

And to top it off, we have the famous quote by very, very Special Agent Bob Ricks as fire consumed Mt. Carmel, "Oh, my God, they're killing themselves."

In recent years the Federal government has adopted an approach in its methods of allowing media coverage of its actions to be strictly controlled. The U.S. invasion of Grenada appears to have been the trial run for this policy. The invasion of Iraq fine-tuned the approach.

The form used by the FBI in its handling of the Waco assault (not the form used by Treasury) reflected this same approach. Only this time, this approach was used against Amerikan Citizens, and the Amerikan press. If we use the response Amerikans reflected to the FBI, by letting that agency treat us as they did during the 51 day stand-off, as a yardstick to measure the remaining backbone the citizenry possess in standing up to law enforcement abuse, we're found severely wanting.

Ultimately, the truth of the fire's origins, and the events leading up to it, will only be revealed on Judgment Day. But facts that have come out since April 19, 1993, cast more than a shadow over the official government version.

At 6 a.m. that morning, Parkland Memorial Hospital in Dallas, received a call from the FBI asking how many beds were available in their burn unit. Parkland would receive and treat, five Davidians surviving the fire.

Based on this call from the FBI, and the FBI's refusal to pay the $350,000 bill, Parkland has brought suit for non-payment, claiming the FBI was the party in obligation, since they knew of the liklihood of the fire in advance, even making arrangements in advance.

In the aftermath of the fire, an "independent" investigator was appointed to pinpoint the source of the fire. The person chosen was Paul Gray, a former ATF employee. At the time of his appointment, his wife was still employed by the Houston office. Gray attended one of the funerals of one of the slain agents.

Appointing someone with obvious connections to one of the parties involved in the conflict, and asking them to render an opinion as to who started the fire, is very revealing as to the precariousness of the FBI's standing with regard to who may have started the fire.

Who had the most to gain by Mt. Carmel being torched? At trial in San Antonio, the government was at a loss to explain the disappearance of the metal door Koresh was standing behind when the ATF began their "dynamic entry." Dick DeGuerin, Koresh's attorney during the 51 day stand-off, stated the door had a number of bullet holes in it, all coming from outside the building.

Jack Zimmerman, the other attorney allowed into Mt. Carmel during the stand-off, toured the structure before the fire and described the roof as looking like "Swiss cheese." This tends to corroborate the Davidians' claim that the National Guard helicopters were shooting through the roof during the initial raid.

Attorney DeGuerin was anxious to end the stand-off so the legal issues raised by government conduct, could be litigated in court. He knew he would win (Source: Parade Magazine, February 27, 1994). The fire destroyed the evidence DeGuerin would have used to prove his case.

The Justice Department Report On Waco that I've continued to extract from, failed to interview DeGuerin. Given the privity of information DeGuerin obtained from Koresh while the stand-off was in progress, it is unconscionable that he wasn't interviewed by the Justice Department.

The fire occurred on Monday. The following Saturday, Paul Gray asked both Dick DeGuerin and Jack Zimmerman to help in the investigation of the fire. Gray's report was to be released the following Wednesday. DeGuerin and Zimmerman were scheduled to leave for Waco Sunday evening at 6:30 p.m.

Once it was confirmed that Gray had been a de facto ATF agent, both attorneys refused to lend their credibility to the report unless asked to participate by the Texas Rangers.

In response, Gray called an unscheduled press conference that same day, and announced that the fire was started by the "cultists." Shortly afterward, the site was bulldozed, hence, the truth was fcrever clouded. Had the truth exonerated the government, the government wouldn't have <u>intentionally</u> clouded the truth. Had citizens been in charge of the dozers they would have been chargeable with obstruction of justice.

Zimmerman has been unrelenting in his open criticism of government handling of events related to the Waco assault. DeGuerin has been somewhat more reserved. Not long after Waco faded from national prominence in the mainstream media, DeGuerin found himself defending Texas U.S. Senator Kay Baily Hitchison on charges of campaign contribution misconduct.

Trial was set but the judge presiding over the case, dismissed the case against her on a pre-trial motion delivered to the court by DeGuerin. Was there a possible connection between this most unique, and highly unusual ruling, and DeGuerin's apparent willingness to keep a low profile concerning his knowledge of the Waco fiasco?

With all of the whitewashing and glaring,

glaring, nakedness of foul play reflected by government officials and those in charge of disseminating information that would enlighten the American public about the Federal government's true motives for invading Mt. Carmel, I marvel at the fact no one with inside information has stepped forward. The best we can get is a top government official to resign, without copping.

On January 27, 1994, approximately two weeks into the trial of the 11 Branch Davidians, Philip Heymann, the No. 2 official in the Justice Department under Janet Reno, resigned. Heymann was in charge of The Justice Department Report On Waco. He stated the reason for his resignation was "bad chemistry" between himself and Reno.

Legal analysis by those with a finger on the pulse of events in the Justice Department, are saying that feminist appointments to positions in the Justice Department are threatening many areas of established law within the Justice Department (Source: Court T.V., September 11, 1994, Washington Review).

The sexual proclivities of David Koresh and his patriarchial approach to life at Mt. Carmel, finds no support within feminism, and his Christian theology is seen by feminism as despicable, its adherents in need of deprogramming.

This feminist infiltration of the Justice Department may have been the "chemistry" Heymann was referring to when he resigned. Certainly, no help would be forth coming to Davidians caught in a legal crossfire.

Heymann listed as his accomplishments while Deputy Attorney General, the settlement of the BCCI banking scandal. Again, the funding of Iraq and the outrageous conduct of the Bush Administration in covering up their evil deeds via the Justice Department stonewalling was absent from Heymann's list.

Heymann quit the Justice Department at the beginning stages of the trial of the 11 Branch Davidians. Maybe the "chemistry" of his conscience got to him.

The format of the trial, given the blessing of U.S. District Judge Walter S. Smith Jr., would ensure only intervention from heaven could get the Davidians justice.

Judge Smith, himself just cleared by Justice Department investigators of allegations he gave perjured testimony against a political opponent in a trial three years prior to the Davidian trial, would rule against the defense in critical areas throughout the trial, that the defense wisely ended its testimony and closed after a mere two days.

Preposterous!! Terry Moran, commentator for Court T.V., upon hearing Judge Smith refuse to allow the jury to hear the emergency 911 call the Davidians made to the Sheriff's Department two minutes into the February 28, assault on Mt. Carmel, asked his reporter on the scene in San Antonio, "Is this a railroad job, or what?"

Smith would allow the 11 defense attorneys 1/2 hour each to deliver their closing arguments. How would Philip Heymann feel, were he facing life in prison for allegedly killing four federal agents, and his attorney was given 30 minutes to tell the jury how the testimony of 138 witnesses, 130 from the prosecution side, proved his client innocent of murder and conspiracy to commit murder. Those were only two of the ten counts against each Davidian. Thirty minutes for closing arguments in a case of this nature, despicable!! More than despicable. I will tell the Federal Government stooge reading this page, I will remain alienated from this "system of justice" until those with power to alter this travesty, this utter tyranny, stand up and remove the mask from the criminal proceeding that took place in San Antonio, and give these human beings their human rights back.

Three of the Davidians, Paul Fatta, Woodrow Kendrick, and Norman Allison, were not even present during the February 28, assault. To allow these three to be included in the murder and conspiracy to commit murder charges, Judge Smith had to broadly interpret a rule of law under the Pinkerton rule that dates back to 1946, and allows a defendant to be convicted even though absent from the scene, at the time the offense was allegedly committed.

Smith hadn't even decided whether the defense could use self-defense as a defense, until the trial had ended. Thanks, asshole.

Week after Nazi tribunal week, the prosecution would offer up witnesses to testify, that, very often, had changed their testimony two or three times prior to taking the witness stand. For example, Roland Ballesteros, the ATF agent claiming to be the first one charging at the front door with a Winchester 12-gauge pump shotgun pointing at the front door, said he saw Koresh and two others standing next to Koresh, none of the three with weapons visible. "I looked up and yelled, 'Police! Lay down!' I yelled it pretty loudly. I yelled, 'Search warrant!', a couple of times. I kept running toward the front door."

Ballesteros continues, "Koresh responded, 'What's going on?', I yelled, 'Search warrant! Lay down'."

On cross-examination, Ballesteros admitted that in a statement to Texas Rangers 10 days after the raid, and in a preliminary hearing in the fall of 1993, he made no mention of anyone yelling anything about police or a search warrant. Ballesteros indicated in his first two accounts that the first shots were fired by ATF, probably by the team assigned to shoot the dogs. The Davidians' female dog and four pups were in a pin in front of Mt. Carmel.

ATF agent Eric Evers was the second government witness to change his story about who fired first. Both Evers and Ballesteros told Texas Rangers in a tape-recorded statement, made right after the assault, that the first shots came from a member of the dog team.

Evers also testified on the stand, that Livingston Fagan shot him as he rounded the north rear corner of Mt. Carmel. In two prior statements, Evers never claimed he could identify the person who shot him.

During Evers testimony, the first of several prosecution failures to turn over key evidence to the defense came to light. A photo lineup shown to Evers (and hidden from the defense) was handed over in court by Texas Ranger Sgt. Ray Cano, the Ranger remarking, "Right is right." On the photo lineup, next to Fagan's picture, Evers had written and initialed the statement that he was "unsure if I.D. is from TV or memory." Fagan was one of 15 black males living at Mt. Carmel, but the only one to exit during the stand-off. It was after

Evers, watching CNN, saw Fagan exit, that he then accused Fagan of shooting him.

Most of the exculpatory evidence showing the Davidians acted in self-defense, was excluded by the judge. The 911 tape of Harvard lawyer Wayne Martin calling the Sheriff's Office during the first minutes of the shootout was excluded. Judge Smith called it self-serving. Only a moron would fail to realize that most any credible evidence tending to prove one acted in self-defense, will be self-serving.

Martin can be heard on the tape saying, "There are 75 men surrounding our building, here at Mt. Carmel, and they're shooting at us." Deputy Sheriff Lynch, who took the call, could be heard on the tape saying, "More than that," as Martin gave the number of agents shooting at Mt. Carmel.

When Lynch asked, "Who fired first?" over the Davidians' speaker phone, two voices were heard responding almost simultaneously, "They did!" The two voices have since been identified as Wayne Martin and Steve Schneider, both now fried beyond recognition.

Other parts of the tape have Martin quoted, "Another chopper with more people, more guns going off. Here they come back. They're firing." Under the Federal Rules of Evidence, 803, 804(b), the 911 tape falls under the Hearsay Rule. But since the Hearsay Rules would include at least three exceptions to the Hearsay Rule that would allow this tape into evidence, the proper objection wasn't raised by the prosecution, because even asshole Smith would have been bound to overrule such an objection. Smith disallowed the tape, looking like a fool to even the greenest of law students, and putting forth his best effort to blindfold justice and the jury.

But the coup de grace for those of us wanting to know the raw truth about why four young agents were used as cannon fodder, and over 90 U.S. Citizens treated like mice in a government sponsored research project, came to light when the conversations, sounds, and schrieks, recorded by several FBI eavesdropping devices, were played to see if Judge Smith would allow the jury to hear what April 19, 1993, sounded like inside Mt. Carmel.

On April 19, the day of the fire, unnerving, vibrating, tanks can be heard crushing wooden walls and knocking down staircasing, then spraying flammable, poisonous chemicals inside. But on this tape you don't hear a voice at the end singing, "Dow, lets you do great things."

No. Not on this tape. On this tape you hear men and women sending up fervent prayers to their creator. Little children are heard crying for their moms and dads. And occasionally a loud-speaker booms the voice of another very, very, special agent, Byron Sage, droning repeatedly, "This is not an assault. This is not an assault."

Needless to say, Judge Smith didn't allow any of it to be heard by the jury. Thomas Jefferson must be turning over in his grave. Only those U.S. Citizens with hearts of stone, who believe the end justifies the means, wouldn't be ashamed to place their hands over their hearts, in the presence of kids at a baseball game, and complete the pledge, "with liberty and justice for all."

The judge also didn't let the jurors hear the tapes made by eavesdropping devices the day before the fire. That was the day Davidians discussed spreading fuel around the Mt. Carmel Center. But, as these and other tapes make clear, the goal wasn't suicide, but a last ditch effort to defend themselves and try to set fire to the tanks. And since the FBI knew this, makes the issue of who lit the fire moot, and makes the FBI's decision to launch an attack look even more <u>RECKLESS</u>. Or more <u>CALCULATED</u>.

The FBI claimed its electronic surveillance devices inside Mt. Carmel, malfunctioned four minutes before the fire started. Calling this trial a "railroad" is an insult to those judges who, in the past, have been meticulous and detailed in their railroading of defendants. This was done by people in San Antonio, who know how to make salsa, but could take a lesson from those in New York City, who can't make salsa, but can railroad the defendants in the World Trade Center bombing and at least make it believable.

Judge Smith, with all his conniving, scaley-skinned facial expressions cleaving to his P.M.S. persona, and the prosecution hiding the videotapes of the crucial encounters between federal agents and the inhabitants of Mt. Carmel, tapes we all know, in our heart of hearts, the feds have. Even after all this bullshit, THEY STILL COULDN"T CONVINCE THE JURY. Had to be Devine intervention.

As I watched Court TV Thursday, February 17, 1994, Sarah Toma, their reporter in San Antonio, announced the defense had rested after two days. TWO DAYS!!! I was shocked. I knew, just knew, the defense attorneys had sold out to the Feds.

I looked out the sliding glass door of my little cabin, watching the blue-green water of the Eel River flow past my property. I began to reflect on my brief experience working for the Sacramento County Public Defender's Office.

For almost two years I had worked in the Municipal Courts, under the supervision of a Supervising Attorney, doing in-court plea bargains for indigent defendants accused of crimes. It was assembly-line justice at its best.

Clients would be transported from their jail cells to court through underground halls. Many times there would be as many as five defendants on the stairs leading to the courtroom. Me and my cohorts would have already convinced many of them, after we had read the police report detailing their alleged offense, that if a jury heard the evidence, a jury would believe the police.

Most of the time, these defendants were ready to plead guilty, their names not yet called by the judge. Once a client remarked that he felt like he was at an auction, but this time, he was the item being bargained for.

I reflected on the course I had taken in law school dealing with Codes of Professional Conduct lawyers are required to conform to. The Code requires lawyers to give their clients a "zealous defense" in a criminal case. I wondered how 11 defendants, charged with 10 separate counts each, and including murder and conspiracy to commit murder, could get a zealous defense in two days.

More painful, and I mean PAINFUL, how could

a nation of lawyers, more experienced and with a deeper knowledge of the law than me, stand by and not raise a voice in protest?? How could this be?

I glanced at my girlfriend. I said, "Someone has to go down there, and help those people."

Within minutes I had loaded up my pick-up with the basics to make the trip to San Antonio. Out the door, as an after thought, I grabbed a blue sport coat. Little did I realize I would be refused entry to the Federal Court in San Antonio without it. Little did I realize this journey would forever change my understanding of how far our system of government has devolved from the principles of justice that has been our nation's bedrock and foundation for over 200 years.

THE VERDICT AND ITS AFTERMATH:

FEDS SPIN OUT OF CONTROL

As I drove further from my home in northern California, I made contact with gas station attendants, store clerks, waitresses, and plain, everyday people. It dawned on me just how oblivious these folks were to the events going on in San Antonio. Few even knew there was a trial going on.

When I reached Bakersfield, California, it was past mid-night. I picked up an interview on my radio between a talk-show host and a woman named Linda Thompson. I had first been apprised of Mrs. Thompson through a movie she had made about the government handling of events that had transpired at Mt. Carmel, and the government's subsequent handling of the event. Her film has footage showing a tank exiting Mt. Carmel, flames coming out of what appears to be a flame thrower.

She has subsequently made an updated version titled, "Waco, The Big Lie, Part II." As I listened to this interview, it became apparent that Linda Thompson had in-depth knowledge of many areas of government activities.

Like myself, she also was a law school graduate. She would become somewhat of a spokesperson for what is becoming known as "The Patriot Movement."

There are a number of individuals scattered across the country, involving themselves with government activity, producing various news letters, radio shows, and slowly moving into cable and satellite television. Their politics, generally, reflect a far right-wing appeal.

The constituents are, basically, salt of the earth, working-class folks, that sense they are getting the "grease job" from the country's leaders, but are having difficulty knowing which buttons to push to get relief. The Machiavellian approach to the masses to, "keep them satisfied and stupified," is now only partially applicable to these folks. They're no longer satisfied, but they still are stupified.

The leaders of this "movement" haven't removed my cynicism and basic view that our government is very tuned-in to political action groups that threaten, or may threaten, its future plans in terms of what direction the government wants to take its governed. I strongly believe those in power will get in on the ground floor of any political movement that may obtain an impact on the way people think.

Linda Thompson has a curious background. Low and behold, she was born in Atlanta. Let's see, the Waco-Herald Tribune, the paper contacted by the ATF and promised "front-row seats" during the Mt. Carmel raid, was owned by Cox Enterprises, from Atlanta. Charles Rochner, Cox' security chief, and the man invited by ATF to observe the ATF exercises at Ft. Hood two days prior to the February 28, 1993, raid, was working out of the Atlanta headquarters. The bank used by the Italian government to help finance the illegal buildup of Iraq's military (and lead to the bombing of the World Trade Center) was its Atlanta branch. The CNN reporters that claimed they saw 20-25 Branch Davidians exit the rear of Mt. Carmel during the April 19 fire, work for Turner Broadcasting, from Atlanta. The Senate Armed Services Committee Chairman, Sam Nunn, is from Atlanta. Newt Gingrich, the new House Majority Leader, he's from Atlanta. And to season that paranoia with a dash of humor, President Carter's late brother Billy, wouldn't you know, from Atlanta.

The 40ish Linda Thompson's parents both worked for the military-industrial complex as Linda grew up, being employed by Lockheed (Source: Interview on radio station KDNO, Delano, California, November 10, 1993).

In the military from 1974-1978, active Army as the Assistant to the Commanding General with Allied Forces in Central Europe, she claims she was the first woman to win the international shooting contest while in the military.

Linda says she only worked with four-star and five-star Generals while being stationed in Europe as the Assistant to the Commanding General of Allied Forces, basically, in charge of NATO. Her task was to revise the NATO War Plans Manual, coordinating Colonels and Lt. Colonels internationally.

Linda's first year in the military, 1974, was the year the Vietnam War officially ended. That was the same year I moved up to the more remote stretches of northern California. I was fed up (no pun intended) with lots of things: the government, Republicans, fast food, commuter traffic, myself. I was 26 years old and suffering overload of available options. But the last option, by far, on my list in 1974, was Linda Thompson's first option exercised.

The year 1974 saw Watergate, Nixon resigning,

Daniel Ellsberg shares the Pentagon Papers, and Linda Thompson wants to join the team that brought us Vietnam, live on TV each night.

Linda has been privy to information not attainable to others. She has made some far-reaching accusations about the inhabitants of Mt. Carmel, from claiming Koresh allowed fugitives to come and go freely, gun-running by Davidians, and she even claims some of the survivors of the April 19 fire, are government agents (Source: Interview on KMUD radio, May 6, 1994, with David Thibodeau, one of the nine survivors, in Garberville, California).

She has been at the forefront in focusing attention on law enforcement misconduct in the handling of events in Waco. She is the darling of the "Patriot Movement" alluded to above. But if the Feds wanted a pipeline to keep tabs on both sides of the Waco issues, those in support of what the government did and those on the edge of open rebellion, she has been placed in as strategic a position as she occupied during her Army stint in Europe. And at $20.00 per videotape, she is making a killing being so altruistic. She was allegedly selling copies of the first Seal Koresh made during the stand-off for $20.00 a pop. So it goes.

I reached San Antonio Sunday evening, February 20, 1994, two days before closing arguments were to begin. I made a beeline for the local newspaper rack. The area I lived in, in northern California, had virtually no coverage of the trial. I'm talking San Francisco Chronicle, Santa Rose Press-Democrat, Sacramento Bee, papers with large circulations.

The largest circulation paper in San Antonio,

the San Antonio Express-News, had a Sunday article laying out the issues the jurors must decide. It took up a full page and included an article, within the same page, about a woman that had escaped a "cult" she claimed had brainwashed her, and taken all her worldly goods. If any of the jurors had read the Express-News over the weekend, this article appeared to give them that last little nudge, in case judge Smith's rulings that had kept out exculpating evidence might not have been sufficient to shield them from the facts.

I learned from some of the locals that entry to the courtroom was on a first-come-first-serve basis. I made sure I was first in line Tuesday morning, only to discover upon attempting to enter, males must wear a sport coat. I ran back to my pick-up and retreived my blazer.

When I was doing in-court plea-bargains, my clients desiring to enter a plea were required to, on the record in open court, give up certain constitutional rights before their pleas could be accepted by the judge. One right they gave up was the right to a jury trial open to the public.

This is a very basic right designed by our founding fathers to ensure against judicial tyranny. The type of tyranny judge Smith had gotten away with during the trial.

I now began to realize how judge Smith and the corporate media had succeeded, lawfully, to excise the Sixth Amendment right to a jury trial, a PUBLIC JURY TRIAL.

The sixth Amendment provides that "in all criminal prosecutions, the accused shall enjoy the right to a...public trial..." The right to a public trial is rooted in the traditional Anglo-American distrust of secret trials, and its purposes are to safeguard against any attempt to employ the courts as instruments of persecution and to inform the public of governmental actions against citizens.

Of the available seats in the San Antonio Federal Courtroom, approximately seventy, the press was given priority. Whatever was left, if any, would be given to those wishing to view the proceedings. I estimated approximately twenty seats remained after the press passes were handed out.

I submit to you a truth based on my San Antonio experience. In modern society, the only way our sixth Amendment right to a public trial can be implimented in a trial setting where the government's credibility is an element inclusive in the proceedings, the defendant should have the right to have TV cameras in the courtroom if he desires, and if the case has such notoriety that networks desire to televise the trial. My fellow Amerikans would be shocked had they been able to view on television, the travesty of justice that took place in San Antonio under our collective noses. Judge Smith may have been lynched for his part, were he to have proceeded as he did in front of a national television audience.

I saw familiar media faces in the courtroom lobby as I stood in line waiting to gain entry. CBS correspondent Vicky Maybrey walked in front of me to enter the women's restroom.

I remember Vicky standing in front of the camera three months after the April 19 fire, a bull-dozer in the background destroying evidence as it "smoothed over" the remains of Mt. Carmel. Vicky told us the government feared tourists might fall in one of the underground bunkers, and didn't want anyone injured. Didn't want a tourist to turn an ankle where over 80 humans were barbequed.

Never mind the chainlink fence surrounding the place with two around-the-clock guards placed inside the fence to guard the true evidence of the Feds' sordid acts. Vicky's in San Antonio to keep the public informed, right? They still think we're MORONS!!!

Court TV's Sara Toma was there. And we got her reports on the up-to-the-minute courtroom blow-by-blows. That is, when there wasn't technical difficulties with the transmission. As the trial progressed, Court TV would have almost daily transmission problems of one sort or another. Just coincidence? Hey Vern. This is yo buddy, Earnest. Know what I mean? Duh!

In criminal trials the prosecution gets to do its closing argument first. Then defense. Then prosecution gets to finish by rebutting.

I was seated in the front row, only a three foot high wall separated me from the eleven Davidian defendants and their attorneys. At first it was difficult for me to distinguish between Davidian and attorney. Though I had seen news coverage of the Waco affair and recognized many Davidian faces, some I hadn't seen. Everyone was so well mannered.

That is, until the prosecution and good ole Bill Johnston took the podium. I remember the first Francis Ford Coppola "The Godfather" movie. When Al Pacino, as Michael, the youngest son of Brando, the Godfather, meets the corrupt cop and the tall dark, Sicilian that wanted the mafia to enter the heroin trade? Johnston's physical features were the mirror image of the Sicilian, only much younger.

For the first ten minutes, Johnston droned on about the variety of evidence he and his cohorts had extracted from the numerous witnesses they had called.

It is astounding that the Justice Department took so much time and spent so much money to call so many witnesses, who ultimately shed so little light on the whole sordid affair.

The stand-off cost taxpayers an estimated $13 million, not counting costs incurred by Texas Rangers and an assortment of local public safety agencies. At the time of the verdict, the trial had cost $1.3 million. Still to be tallied were totals for air fare, lodging, and meals for the 130 prosecution witnesses, and hotel bills for the jurors. All this expense, and not one videotape of consequence!!!

Soon Johnston stopped droning about evidence that had, in his opinion, proved the Davidians' guilt. He knew the proof wasn't there, and sensing the jury wasn't buying his bullshit, chose character assassination as the only remaining option, neither the law or the facts being on his side.

Along the way, Johnston called Paul Fatta, one of the defendants not present during the February 28 shootout, a "blood merchant." Apparently, Johnston was referring to the fact that Fatta attended gun shows, legal activities in the U.S. for at least the last

200 years. If Johnston weren't so brainwashed he'd recognize the real blood merchants were those men connected directly and indirectly with the Bush Administration and its clandestine supplying of the Iraqis. True blood merchants indeed.

Johnston then called defendant Kevin Whitecliff "a sniveling coward." Johnston kept referring to his "theory of who was behind the windows" while the shootout continued on February 28. Jeff Kearney, one of the soft spoken defense attorneys, would make Johnston look like the fool that he was, when, during Kearney's 30-minute closing argument, he looked Johnston straight in the eye, the room spooky silent for an extended period, and said, "We don't convict people in this country based on theory."

Johnston topped off his closing argument, which was more a case study in attorney stupidity, by calling the team of defense attorneys "a pack of hyenas."

It took all I could do to restrain myself from leaping over the three-foot wall and giving the son of a bitch what he really had earned since involving himself in the affairs of the folks at Mt. Carmel, starting as far back as June of 1992. Not wanting to harm the chances of the defense, I looked up at the roof and maintained. Had to be Devine intervention.

Johnston finished his allotted time, the noon break came, then the defense, each given 30 minutes, took the podium. Of the eleven defense attorneys I saw and heard, some gave clear indications they had reservations about defending such a crew as these Davidians.

Joe Turner, Ruth Riddle's attorney, referred to Koresh as "a nut." And he said he thought the Davidians started the April 19 fire.

One other attorney, in a half-hearted, less than zealous, hell, less than mild droning, said he couldn't stay for the remaining closing arguments of the remaining attorneys. He had other commitments.

But at least six defense attorneys gave it their best shot. The seventh, Daniel Cogdell, vibrated every brain within earshot.

If you're ever in Texas, and the Federal Government comes to your house, and decides to blow the front door off your place, shoot at you, your wife, and your kids. Then they inject CS gas into the place on those still alive, and burn the place down, if you make it out alive and don't get shot exiting the inferno, when you get to your jail cell, call Dan Cogdell. He'll do you right.

Cogdell said he got a call from Dick DeGuerin to go to Dallas. DeGuerin wanted Cogdell to visit Clive Doyle who was in the burn unit at Parkland Memorial Hospital, to see if Cogdell would consider defending Doyle.

Cogdell said as he passed an assortment of FBI, ATF, Texas Rangers, and law enforcement agents of every description, when he finally got to Doyle's room, he said he found a man with burns from his waist to his ankles, hand-cuffed to a bed, barely able to manuever. He said he instantly chose to take the case. Cogdell said, "This is America. This isn't suppose to happen here."

When Cogdell took the podium, most of the other defense attorneys had closed. Cogdell, friendly, in his mid-thirties, handsome, sort of a Dennis Quaid with a law degree, only Cogdell wasn't acting, he was the real deal.

He started by looking at the jury and telling them, "I've never been so proud to take a podium in all my life. My mentor taught me, 'Never get loud and emotional in front of a jury. It might hurt your client.' I'm going to disregard that advice today." Then Cogdell started to deliver.

He looked Bill Johnston straight in the eye, Johnston being less than ten feet away. Cogdell leaned over to get even closer. He referred to Johnston calling them "hyenas" saying, "Coming from you, Sir, I consider it a high compliment."

Cogdell began to attack "government arrogance....the belief that as long as they have a badge and a gun, they can do anything that they want."

"The law doesn't begin and end at ATF press conferences," he said. He was now raising his voice talking, or more accurately, yelling, face to face with Johnston. Johnston turned slightly to position his body so as to be looking more directly into Cogdell's eyes. Johnston wasn't backing down. He's a true believer.

Judge Smith reached over and turned off Cogdell's microphone. It didn't faze Dan, Cogdell probably expected it, given judge asshole's prior conduct.

For a moment I truly believed Johnston and Cogdell were going to abandon closing arguments in favor of beating the crap out of each other, right there in the Federal

Courtroom. Boom, spin that asshole!!

Miraculously, Cogdell could show this type of genuine anger, and still maintain a clear mind. He screamed, "The ATF acted like a bunch of GI Joes, who raised the blue ATF flag over the ashes of Mt. Carmel, like they've won some sort of war, like they've claimed some sort of victory out of the ashes of 90 burned men, women, and children."

As Cogdell paused to take a breath, the room full of press and spectators could be heard to make an audible group sound, like we all were on an elevator that had just come to an abrupt stop. We were in a courtroom surfing, and Cogdell was allowing us to ride his wave. He was speaking the truth, the reality of what really happened that day of the shootout. He was slapping our faces with the truth, and the pain felt good. For a moment, the months and months of spin had spun out.

I glanced over at the jury to see if I could get a glimpse of what the jurors might be thinking. Body language, any hint. A spanish fellow in the front row, with a goatee. I couldn't believe my eyes. He was looking at Johnston. He was gritting his teeth. He had a look of distain, no, more at outright anger. It was at that moment that I knew the Feds had lost, at least as to the murder and conspiracy to commit murder charges.

Cogdell, unrelenting, pointed to the perversion of language engaged in by the prosecution, to make law enforcement's storm trooper mentality more acceptable to the jury. "What was a flash bang, is now a diversionary device," Cogdell bellowed, referring to agents who testified that the flash-bang grenades hurled into Mt. Carmel were harmless. "What was an explosion, is now a rapid expansion of gases," he continued. "What was a tank track, is now a ground disturbance. What was an assault...is now a lawful execution of a search warrant." A few snickers could be heard from the artists scetching the courtroom scene in the front row to my left.

Returning to Bill Johnston's Tuesday "pack of hyenas" description of the team of defense attorneys, he said, "Mr. Johnston, frankly, an insult from you, sir, is the highest compliment I've been paid. Given what you did out there that day...I embrace your hostility."

A half-hour goes quick. Cogdell finished by criticizing the government prosecution team for not calling to the stand critical witnesses like ATF leaders and case agent Davy Aguilera, who sat with prosecutors throughout the trial. Aguilera, you recall, was the lead agent in investigating Koresh and his followers.

"Where is Byron Sage, head negotiator for the FBI?" Cogdell asked. "Do you think maybe you people had the right to hear from Sage, Sarabyn, Chojnacki, and Aguilera? The government owes you more." Cogdell pointed out that not one government witness testified that there was a conspiracy.

Cogdell chided prosecutors for painting the defendants with a broad brush. "The Mona Lisas, the true works of art, aren't painted with a roller," he said.

"A blanket conviction of everybody at that table will give law enforcement a blank check," he said. "It will give everybody with a badge and a gun---from a Wackenhut security guard to Janet Reno---the authority to do whatever they want, to whomever they want, however they want."

Judge Smith, anxious to get Cogdell shut down, called time on him. Defense attorney Mike DeGuerin jumped up and shouted, "He can have five minutes of my time." The room turned chimerical.

Smith, as well as most of us in the room, was dumbfounded. He looked over at the wall, and in a voice almost inaudible, said, "Continue on."

I felt tears welling up in my eyes. Tears of shame that the justice system of my country had been cheapened, and lowered to such a level. Tears of anger that these eleven people might be placed behind bars for an extended period of time, with genuine criminals, the father-raping kind.

Tears of frustration and powerlessness to stop this train of tyranny that has such a head of steam.

I can't remember, can't recall that last five minutes DeGuerin gave Cogdell to finish his closing. I doubt even the jury remembers. It should have ended as Austin defense attorney Gerry Morris quietly pleaded with the jury in behalf of his client.

Wrinkled up, old man Woodrow Kendrick, began to weep as Morris closed, "All I ask you for is his liberty---what God gave him," Morris said. "And all I want to do is drive him home."

When the jury came back into court February 26, 1994, with the verdicts, Morris indeed, would be able to drive Woodrow Kendrick home. And Cogdell could do the same for Clive Doyle, his client. Both were found innocent of all charges. As were Ruth Riddle and Norman Allison. Or so it seemed.

In judge Smith's instructions to the jury, the conspiracy charge was referred to as "Count One", the murder charge as "Count Two". A charge defined as "using and carrying a firearm during and in relation to the commission of an offense", was termed "Count Three".

The defendants couldn't be found guilty of Count Three without first being found guilty of Count One. Smith was basically telling the jurors that Count One (conspiracy) was a left shoe, and Count Three was the matching right shoe. The jurors were to pair the shoes, or issue a bare verdict of not guilty.

As soon as Smith saw that the jury had found all eleven Davidians innocent of Count One, but six of them guilty of Count Three, he gave out a long and audible sigh, and called both prosecution and defense teams to the bench. Johnston's team wanted him to send Count Three back to the jurors for rectification. The defense wanted him to throw out the finding, to dismiss it. "The court will set that finding aside," he ruled, explaining the only rectification he expected from the jury would be not guilty on Count Three, were he to send it back.

Pandimonium? Sure. Partying? March 2, 1994, backstage after a Texas Independence Day gig in Austin, the ever-credible Willie Nelson, singer/songwriter deluxe, congratulated several Branch Davidian defense attorneys celebrating with Willie backstage.

I can imagine Willie getting them in a one-on-one at some point, and getting to the bone of what guys like Cogdell knew about the case, that never came out at trial, or anywhere else, for that matter.

Willie had a t-shirt on backstage that said "Down With Nazi Mentality." Were Willie inclined to pen lyrics to a song that told the truth about Waco, he could have a devastating impact on a large number of folks that may have swallowed the government line about Waco.

Within a month of this gig, Willie Nelson was arrested sleeping alongside the road in his Mercedes. Nelson told the arresting officers fatigue had overcome him and he pulled over to rest. The "evil weed" was allegedly found in his car and Willie taken to jail.

The March 2 celebration quickly turned to a bad hangover that wouldn't go away. On March 7, 1994, judge Smith issued a post-trial ruling, re-instating guilty verdicts on the weapons charge against seven of the eleven defendants. Six of the seven had faced maximum 10-year sentences. The seventh, Ruth Riddle, had been acquitted of all charges. Now she and the others faced between 30-40 years in prison.

Mommas don't let your babies grow up to be Davidians!! But if they do, don't let them be sentenced in judge Smith's court. If any doubt remained that judge Smith was taking orders from Janet Reno, and ilk recruited into the Justice Department by her, Smith's logic in sentencing the Davidians to the maximum, would remove it.

"These defendants, and other adult Branch

Davidians, engaged in a conspiracy to cause the deaths of federal agents," Smith spewed. Smith was referring to Count One, to which the jury acquitted all eleven defendants. "By its verdict, convicting the defendants of violating Section 924(c)(1)---Count Three---the jury found that they were members of a conspiracy to murder federal agents," he spun. A magician with words, he ain't.

Smith found that "by a combination of suicide and murder inflicted by Davidian upon Davidian, all but a handful of the Davidians were killed." In essence, he found the eight defendants in front of him guilty of setting the fire, yet when Mt. Carmel was consumed by fire, three of the defendants were already in jail, and a fourth was in hiding!! Why was a charge of felony-murder (alleging arson related deaths) never brought?

According to Federal Sentencing Law, type of weapon used in the re-instated Count Three, would determine the number of years the defendants would serve in prison. Defense attorneys argued that juries, not judges, must determine what type of weapon, if any, the defendants were guilty of using, a question of fact, not of law, that only a jury can legally decide.

It was becoming painfully obvious that re-instating Count Three would open the flood gates of Appeal to higher authority, but judge Smith was irrepressible.

He had disbanded the jury at the end of the trial, and recalling them wasn't possible, hence, Judge Smith chose to circumvent the law and decide for the jury, what type of weapon the Davidians used in the crime the jury said they didn't commit. Has your gray matter begun to drip out the side of your ear yet?

Using a drug merchant analogy, judge Smith decided that all Davidians had "constructive possession" of automatic weapons, and that access to such weapons constitutes their "use."

"When a drug merchant stocks his home with a supply of weapons, federal courts regard that home as a fortress, the purpose of the weapons to further the illegal activity," he spun. He said the Davidians lived in "not only a figurative but literal fortress," whose purpose was to murder ATF agents.

Now, through the sophistry only students of "law" can truly see through, Smith had placed automatic weapons in the hands of people the jury had already acquitted, and having equated the vegetarian, celibate, non-smoking, clean-living, drug-free Davidians with the Medellin Cocaine Cartel, Smith had effectively "greased" the defendants. Now he would attempt to penetrate their spirit.

He ordered five of the Davidians---Brad Branch, Kevin Whitecliff, Jamie Castillo, Livingston Fagan, and Renos Avraam, to prison for 40 years!! FORTY UCKIN YEARS!!!!!!

They got ten for aiding and abetting involuntary manslaughter, a charge the jury found them guilty of. They got three times that much for Count Three, the count Smith dismissed and re-instated.

Smith sentenced Paul Fatta to 15 years, claiming it was obvious to Smith and the prosecutors, that Fatta was part of the conspiracy the jurors said didn't exist. Ruth Riddle got "only" five years for the Count Three fiasco.

She was, at one point, 30 minutes from a plane ramp heading to Canada. Graime Craddock got 10 years for possessing a hand grenade, plus "only" ten years for the dubious Count Three. During allocutions, time given defendants to define issues, show remorse, or defiance, neither Riddle nor Craddock had spoken in defiance of judge Smith's "Smoke, Wind, and Fire, Magic Sentencing Show."

The remaining six Davidians, during allocutions, remained constant, maintaining as Livingston Fagan, the former Professor of Theology and Ordained Minister eloquently told judge Smith, "We are innocent, absolutely, without doubt." Apparently, Smith hadn't been able to penetrate the spirit.

During a prison interview after sentencing, Fagan, now ever-vulnerable, adamantly laid it on the line: "The death of David Koresh will not mean the end of the Branch Davidian religion," Fagan said. "He was merely a mouthpiece for the spirit that was leading us. That which was leading us, is in us. It is not a case of our being lead as a group. We are individuals, like you people. Every so often, we have a Coke. We like ice-cream. We take our kids for a walk. But everyone is led by a spirit that is within them," he said.

"If you read the Scriptures, it is not about external government. The whole process of God is that you have individuals who govern themselves. If you live in righteousness with God, you don't need an external power. But when you lose that internal reality of self-control, then that void is replaced by an external government, which is what you are seeing right now in the U.S," he said.

Internal reality of self-control? Void being replaced by an external government? Is Professor Fagan for real? Or are these deep thoughts by Jack Handey? Lets look closer.

EXTERNAL GOVERNMENT CONTROL:

DOES THE END JUSTIFY THE MEANS?

Distant ships sailing in the mist
You were born with a snake in both your fists
While a hurricane was blowing.
Freedom just around the corner from you.
But with the truth so far off
What good would it do.
(Bob Dylan, from Jokerman, off the Infidels album)

There is Dylan singing happy birthday to the position of Pontiff.

Throughout this ordeal I've maintained that the ATF raid on Mt. Carmel February 28, 1993, was executed for reasons other than those officially given by the Treasury Department, concurred in by the Justice Department, and to a large degree, most all other governing bodies charged with duties to respond.

As Professor Fagan stated above, voids or vacuums in one's personal life, are filled by external government to maintain stability. And so it is with relations between nations. Filling vacuums in power is constant and ongoing, to maintain stability at best, to assert and increase power, at worst.

Were those in charge of U.S. foreign affairs to come clean and expose the raw truth about the Iraqi military build-up, Banco del Lavoro Nazionale, Desert Storm, the World Trade Center bombing, and the "dynamic entry" diversion at-all-costs Waco tirade, like the true believers they are, they'd say, "Yes, and if I had to, I'd do it again."

When the Reagan Administration took Iraq

off its list of terrorist nations in 1984, thus allowing Iraq to qualify for U.S. foreign assistance, the motives were to try and avoid allowing any one country to dominate the region. Funding Iraq's military, allowed Iraq to battle its arch-rival Iran, on even terms.

The U.S. National Security Council (the current President at any given time ruling the NSC is immaterial), since the early 80's, is convinced the greatest threat to peace in the Middle East prior to and after Desert Storm, isn't Iraq but the Islamic fundamentalist government in Iran.

Not only does Iran openly call for the destruction of Israel, it advocates the overthrow of the governments of the moderate Arab states; such as Egypt, Kuwait, and Saudi Arabia, and establishing in their place, Islamic fundamentalist governments answering solely to Tehran (Source: From the Congressional Record by various Committee Chairmen, Congressmen, Senators, on almost daily basis, to Conservative Think Tank IDC'S DEFENSE-LINK).

If Iran succeeded in controlling large amounts of Middle Eastern oil, coupled with its continuing military growth, dire consequences might ensue. The growth of Iranian influence raises substanial concerns within the NSC.

I'd have fewer doubts about NSC credibility with regard to its fears of Iranian potential, had not those involved in the Iraqi build-up made so much damn money by promoting such a policy. Bush signing eleven waivers for his cabinet members' conflicts of interest, so they could partake in planning and carrying out, Iraqi foreign policy, reeks of ulterior, impure motives.

Monetary temptations aside, profound changes have occurred with regard to Middle East peace and Israel's willingness to bend. Breaking down the Berlin Wall and the end of the so-called "cold war", have created various voids and vacuums alluded to earlier.

The nation that officially housed the Banco del Lavoro Nazionale and used its Atlanta branch to clandestinely help supply financing to the Iraqis, formed its first right-wing government, complete with neo-fascist Cabinet members. Billionaire media mogul and neo-fascist Silvio Berlusconi, became Prime Minister of Italy in April 1994.

I wouldn't bore you with necessary details of Italian politics, but House Banking Committee Chairman Henry Gonzalez failure to pierce the Justice Department armor protecting the Bush Administration from exposure for its BNL activities, is directly related to Italian banking's incestuous relationship with high government officials.

Berusconi's corporation, Fininvest, dominates the worlds of private television, publishing, retailing, and even soccer. Without the influence of Bettino Craxi, Italy's former Socialist Party leader, now hiding out in Tunisia as a fugitive from justice, Berlusconi wouldn't have been allowed to build his web of T.V. stations, newspapers, and magazines that made him Italy's Super Spinmeister, the Latin Lathario of Narcissistic Newspeak.

During the 1980's, in the U.S. under the Reagan and Bush "guardianship" that allowed the deregulation of our Savings and Loans, and their subsequent looting, the same activity was occurring in Italian politics. Berlusconi, during this period, was involved in "P-2", the secret masonic society that included the country's most important businessmen, politicians, generals, and Vatican officials. P-2 has been directly linked to various banking scandals, and a host of other illegal activities in and out of government.

Over 2,000 arrests have been made of participants known in Italy as the Tangentopoli investigations. But to no avail, thus far.

In June of 1994, just after the G-7 meetings (in which Clinton attended), Berlusconi freed roughly 2,000 suspects that had been preventively detained and imposed strict controls on press reports of corruption investigations (Source: The New Republic, Sept. 1994).

All hell broke loose once the Italian public realized what Berlusconi had done. He was forced to back off but the suspects remain free. The magistrates overseeing the Tangentpoli investigations, then arrested Berlusconi's brother and two business associates for bribing treasury officials. Keep in mind that Italy's banking system is government owned, unlike the U.S. system, at least on paper and in theory.

In September 1992, House Banking Committee Chairman Gonzalez placed in the Congressional Record, evidence that top BNL officials knew of, and were willing participants in, the illegal activities of its Atlanta branch.

Two months later, in November 1992, the Italian Senate voted to create a second special commission to look into the BNL scandal.

This Italian Senate Commission's mandate is to probe whether the Italian government acted in concert with the U.S. and British governments, to aid Iraq's military industrialization effort.

When Gonzalez stepped up on the House floor on January 21, 1993, and announced his continued desire to get the records from the new Clinton Administration that had been denied him by the Bushmasters, it must have sent shivers down the backs of government officials in Britain, and Italy, as well as the U.S.

And when, four days later, Gonzalez sent President Clinton a letter requesting the official documents, well, that is when the World Trade Center bombing and Waco began to require lifelong bureaucrats possessing positions of power (that grow larger as U.S. sovereinty continues to dissolve into the New World Order) to ask themselves if the end justifies the means.

Following Gonzalez January 25, 1993, letter to President Clinton requesting official documents mentioned above, he was followed on the House floor by Newt Gingrich, the Republican House Whip from, of all places, Georgia.

Gingrich's job as "whip" is similiar to the role former Boston Celtic hackman Jungle Jim Luscatoff filled during the Celtic hayday in the 1960's, in professional basketball. If the Celtic opponent had a player with a hot hand, coach Red Auerbach would bring in "Jungle Jim". Built like a brick shit-house with a shooting touch to match, when Luscatoff came back to the bench, very often the opponent with the "hot hand" now had a hot "bruised" hand.

Gingrich followed Gonzalez on the House floor to speak about what Gingrich called "Renewing American Civilization." He gave a short outline of Amerika's recent past and issued some juicy quotes regarding what he viewed as Amerika's greatest threat to freedom.

"Today, the greatest threat to freedom is here at home. The decay of Amerikan civilization is undermining our very capacity to have economic productivity, our capacity to have a decent, safe society here at home, our capacity to project assistance abroad to help other people," he said.

Anyone would be hard-pressed to find disagreement with these statements. Now Gingrich turned his focus to Gonzalez desire to unearth the truth concerning BNL and related matters. "To learn to abide by the rules of self-government, that is why the power of last week's inaugural ceremony was so emotional. There is magic to our ability to have one party, one side, in the White House, in the Oval Office with the most powerful military machine in the history of the human race, and magically, at exactly 12 o'clock on January 20, under our Constitution, to transfer that office to the other party," he said.

Gingrich was letting Gonzalez know that, up to this point in time Gonzalez shooting touch had been held in check. But if Gonzalez were to start to get "hot", the Republicans had a "Jungle Jim" in reserve.

Then Gingrich reached the bottom line. "The key question is simply: Does a proposed policy help people become more responsible, more productive, and more safe so they can be prosperous and free, so they can pursue happiness? If the answer is yes, then the proposed policy is constructive. If the answer is no, then it is destructive," he said.

Hey Newt, what if the proposed policy is secret? What if the proposed policy is hatched behind closed doors among a select few "newts" sitting on the National Security Council? And what if the proposed policy helps some and is harmful to others? These types of questions were absent from Gingrich's train of thought.

But recipients of foreign policy decisions hatched behind closed doors, that adversely affect them, have no public forum to debate clandestine policies and violate our form of Constitutional government. Newt supports the GATT treaty. It also violates our Constitution. Keep a close eye on Newt.

Where foreign policy is conducted in the manner reflected by the Bush Administration during its funding of the Iraqi military build-up, such methods give rise to calculated responses that may place respondents behind bars. Such is the case of Jonathan Pollard.

When Jonathan Pollard turned 13, his father took him on a bar mitzvah trip to Europe, to the camps.

They saw Bergen-Belson. And Treblinka. And Auschwitz, where as many as 75 members of their family perished before Jonathan was born.

"Jonathan was named for a little boy who died in Auschwitz," says sister, Carol. "I was named for a young girl who died there. I think we grew up with thosed 75 people on our shoulders" (this writer is beginning to feel the same for the 90 plus Davidians and agents dying at Mt. Carmel).

That says volumes about why Jonathan Pollard, once a civilian employee of U.S. Naval Intelligence, is now a convicted spy. At 40, he is about to begin his 10th year of a life sentence in prison---amid growing protests by those who see his case as an ugly mix of politics, vengence, and perhaps, anti-Semitism.

When the Reagan/Bush era began its clandestine policy involving Iraq, the U.S. withheld from Israel data on the build-up of chemical, biological, and radiological weapons in Iraq. Pollard began giving Israel this withheld information. Arrested in 1985, Pollard agreed to a plea bargain and waive a trial that might have compromised U.S.-Israel interests.

In exchange, prosecutors assured Pollard that he would not receive a life sentence. But on the morning of sentencing, former Defense Secretary Caspar Weinberger is said to have sent the judge a note asking for a harsh penalty. Remember, Weinberger was pardoned by Bush for any role Caspar might have played in Iran-Contra!!

Pollard's first 10 months of imprisonment were spent in a ward for the criminally insane. BEG YOUR PARDON, ASSHOLE!! Pollard contends he gave information to Israel, only after the U.S. stopped honoring a 1983 agreement to share information. Iraq was taken off a list of terrorist nations by the Reagan Administration in 1984.

City councils in Los Angeles, New York, and Chicago have called for Pollard's sentence to be commuted. In Hollywood, actor Jon Voight has joined Whoopi Goldberg, Edward James Olmos, Jack Lemmon, Harrison Ford, Gregory Peck, Barbara Hersey, and others asking for Pollard's sentence to be commuted.

I respect these above mentioned folks concern for the fate of Jonathan Pollard. I would respect them even more if these same folks saw the connection between U.S. foreign policy involving the Iraqi military build-up, the World Trade Center bombing, and the media diversion to Waco, Texas, two days later, under the auspices of the Treasury Department.

Pollard acted in an affirmative manner to alert Israel to a possible threat, the Davidians were used as cannon fodder, matching the necessary profile that would be sufficient to draw and keep, Amerika's attention away from the events Pollard was alerting Israel to, years before the threat evolved into the Persian Gulf War.

We now know Pollard's fears about Israeli security wasn't misplaced. During the Gulf War, Israelis were victims of numerous SCUD missile attacks, and were forced to tape any air leaks in homes and offices, hoping to avoid possible chemical and biological SCUD bombs. Sounds like a 51 day stand-off at Mt. Carmel!! Fewer Israelis died during the Persian Gulf War than Davidians at Mt. Carmel.

Remember Arthur Kent, the SCUD Stud. NBC's version of Mick Jagger doing the nasty with a video-camcorder, live from Riad, Saudi Arabia, during the Persian Gulf War. Kent must have been privy to sensitive information. Another suit settled out of court keeps us from knowing.

Kent was assigned to a war zone in Croatia following the Persian Gulf War. He refused the assignment and was fired, NBC labeling "the Stud" a "coward." Kent, choosing to picket outside the NBC Headquarters, convinced NBC that he, not Mick Jagger, was the true street fighting man. Wisdom told Kent his 30-second news-bite tour should stay out of a fractured country whose government was trying to confiscate and burn, recent pictures of its leaders and Lawrence Eagleburger, then Deputy Secretary Of State, and Eagleburger's "Yugo uck a U.S. bank" routine.

Seeing what Eagleburger had helped bring the Iraqis, Kent chose to try work in Canada, rather than Croatia. NBC would claim Kent couldn't cut the mustard. Kent said he didn't want to breath it.

Vacuums, voids. Yugoslavia, Europe, there all over. Lot of action, more than I've seen in my 47 years. And the Vatican has come out of the closet, figuratively speaking, of course.

Consider, this country, so-called, is 800 square acres of office space in the middle of Rome. Are any of us so gullible we separate Vatican City from Italian politics? If you do, you probably drive a Yugo.

Less than two years after the Israeli citizens had taped their windows in fear of breathing nerve or mustard gas, Israel and The Vatigan formally recognized each other. March 4, 1994, The Vatican would complete establishing diplomatic relations with all the countries that have land borders with Israel.

Its been a couple of tough millennium for Romans and Jews. There are approximately 15 million Jews in the world, compared to almost one billion Catholics. Were I forced to chose sides, my momma always taught me to lend a hand to the underdog.

Some translations of Latin say "Vatican"

translates to English as "divining serpent". Must be potent stuff. Even Aristide, the HooDoo man of Haiti, pays homage.

If you don't get the picture by now, I refuse to stamp it on your forehead. Since I drove to San Antonio and saw that travesty called a trial, I've chosen to disregard the wisdom that says, "Don't be too attached to the outcome." Wisdom from a Zen-yuppie.

You don't think such thoughts if you wake up each morning in a 6 foot by 10 foot cell. In that spot, even Andre Agassi would say, "Outcome, not image, is everything."

As I've aged, lowering my expectations is not only practical, but painful. Those humans that were consumed by flames at Mt. Carmel, and those agents and Davidians that lost their lives during the raid of February 28, 1993, are gone forever. But those eleven Davidians sentenced by judge Smith in San Antonio, are still waking up in a 6 foot by 10 foot cell. STILL!!!!

Civil servants, whether at the Federal, State, or County level, have no credibility, with regard to law enforcement, so long as the Branch Davidian travesty is ignored. My lowered expectations refuse to enter the gutter. I'll die first.

The state of the Union now requires our Federal government to allow television cameras in the courtroom, if requested by any defendant in a criminal trial.

As this book goes to press, the hangover of hiding the facts surrounding the BNL scandal continues to blur our U.S. Citizenry's vision. New Special Prosecutor, Kenneth Starr, taking over for Robert Fiske, has appointed William Duffy, to serve as Starr's deputy overseeing the investigation in Little Rock, Arkansas (President Clinton's base).

And, of course, the ever-present kicker: Duffy was a specialist in complex civil and criminal litigation, including banking law, WHILE A PARTNER AT KING AND SPAULDING IN ATLANTA, BNL'S LAWYERS (Source: Washington Post, Sept. 13, 1994).

Ah yes, King and Spaulding, the lawfirm defending Banco del Lavoro Nazionale (yes, the first four letters spell Nazi). The firm that had assigned Bill Hendricks, the former chief of the Fraud Section of the Justice Department (the Section responsible for signing off on any BNL indictment), the man that had resigned his position at the Justice Department the same day the FBI raided the BNL Atlanta Branch, so Hendricks could defend BNL. Now, King and Spaulding have a partner in Little Rock, Arkansas, overseeing how culpable our current President might prove to be with regard to his Whitewater banking activities. You might say King and Spaulding have the best of both worlds.

As I sit here today, December 4, 1994, putting the finishing touches on this manuscript, I have a new favorite show that comes on my satellite, on G-4 transponder 15 between 9-10 p.m. Its Bob Enyart Live. Its a television call-in talkshow.

Bob recently had a caller tell him she wasn't Christian. She felt religion was a vehicle used by men to control other men. Bob's response was to point out to this caller that men of the Bible, when confronted with their evil deeds, always had to admit them, thereby keeping the path to forgiveness open to themselves. And this admission to wrong-doing allowing the truth to remain the truth without giving in to the temptation to manipulate it.

Our government, with respect to its position in relation to the Branch Davidians, sits in the same position as King David held with respect to Uriah the Hittite.

II Samuel 12:

And the Lord sent Nathan unto David. And he came unto him, and said unto him, "There were two men in one city; the one rich, and the other poor.

The rich man had exceeding many flocks and herds: But the poor man had nothing, save one little ewe lamb, which he had bought and nourished up: and it grew up together with him, and with his children; it did eat of his own meat, and drank of his own cup, and lay in his bosom, and was unto him as a daughter.

And there came a traveller unto the rich man, and he spared to take of his own flock and of his own herd, to dress for the wayfaring man that was come unto him; but took the poor man's lamb, and dressed it for the man that was come to him."

And David's anger was greatly kindled against the man; and he said to Nathan, "As the Lord liveth, the man that hath done this thing shall surely die: And he shall restore the lamb fourfold, because he did this thing, and because he had <u>NO</u> <u>PITY</u>."

And Nathan said to David, "Thou art the man. Thus saith the Lord God of Israel, I annointed thee king over Israel, and I delivered thee out of the hand of Saul; and gave thee thy master's house, and thy master's wives into thy bosom, and gave thee the house of Israel and of Judah; and if that had been too little, I would moreover have given unto thee such and such things.

Wherefore, hast thou despised the commandment of the Lord, to do evil in his sight? Thou hast killed Uriah the Hittite with the sword, and hast taken his wife to be thy wife, and hast slain him with the sword of the children of Ammon.

Now therefore the sword shall never depart from thine house; because thou hast despised me; and hast taken the wife of Uriah the Hittite to be thy wife.

Thus saith the Lord, Behold, I will raise up evil against thee out of thine own house, and will take thy wives from before thine eyes, and give them unto thy neighbor, and he shall lie with thy wives in the sight of this sun. For thou didst it secretly: but I will do this thing before all Israel, and before the sun."

And David said unto Nathan, "I HAVE SINNED AGAINST THE LORD."

EPILOGUE

As this book goes to press lots of action is occurring on the World stage. October 15, 1994, 28 Branch Davidians were buried without ceremony in McLennan County paupers' graves.

David Thibodeau, one of the nine survivors of the April 19, 1993, fire came out to visit me in northern California, and speak at some of the places I reserved for him in Humboldt and Mendocino County.

Some curious happenings took place during this period of time. Thibodeau spoke on the local radio station with this writer hosting a call-in talk show. He and I entered the station approximately 7:00 a.m. May 5, 1994. It was a warm, sunny evening. Within 20 minutes of entering the studio, the radio station was vibrated by an enormous bolt of LIGHTNING!! When you listen to the cassette included with this book you will hear this phenomena. It rained the remainder of the interview. Weird.

Mr. Thibodeau flew back to Houston to meet with Ramsey Clark, the former Attorney General in the Lyndon Johnson Administration, on May 6&7. He flew back to northern California to speak in Garberville, California, on May 8, 1994.

On May 7, 1994, a U.S. Coast Guard helicopter came over my house, located in a sparsely populated area, at an enormous rate of speed, at about tree top level, twice within twenty minutes. Highly unusual, I called the Federal Aviation Administration to make a formal complaint the following Monday, and made a formal complaint to the Humboldt County Sheriff's Office May 9, 1994.

The Coast Guard is part of the Treasury Department's law enforcement section. The pilot of the helicopter, Larry Williams, called me at my house about one hour after he had buzzed my house, admitted he was the pilot, but could give no legitimate reason for doing so.

My plan was to bring suit against the Treasury Department for trespass. Sounds trivial to you? It sounded trivial to me also. Until July 12, 1994, rolled around. That was the date Larry Williams and his same co-pilot died in a crash of the same helicopter out in Shelter Cove, California, approximately 15 miles from my house these guys buzzed two months earlier.

Remember the Green Sweep case I referred to earlier, involving the military landing on the Kings Range to look for marijuana. And the attorney, Ron Sinoway, taking the depositions of high government replicants, then suffering a "stroke." Two days after the Coast Guard helicopter crashed, the law office housing the Green Sweep files was gutted by fire. Isn't this fun.

Of course we have seen the latest election results. We now know the Republicans have control. And if I see Newt Gingrich's face on C-SPAN one more time I'm going to do my best impression of Elvis Presley when he saw Wayne Newton's face appear on his TV. Break out the .357 mag. and do in the set.

Gingrich supported the GATT. And just who is being pushed to head the World Trade Organization, the agency that will administer trade disputes and replace the existing Geneva-based bureaucracy of GATT? The European Union, lead by Germany and France, is backing an Italian diplomat and trade expert, Renato

Ruggiero, who served as the Italian minister of foreign trade from 1987-1991. That is the time frame within which the publicly owned Italian bank, the Banco del Nazionale Lavoro helped finance the Iraqi military buildup. The military buildup that included nerve and mustard gas among its chemical warfare materials. I predict Ruggiero will get the assignment. Hasn't he earned it?

THE DECODED MESSAGE OF THE SEVEN SEALS OF THE BOOK OF REVELATION

by

DAVID KORESH

Sunday, April 17, A.D. 1994

"Day of Information"

EDITORIAL PREFACE

On Wednesday, April 14th, following the eight day Passover celebration David Koresh released what turned out to be his final letter through his lawyer, Dick DeGuerin. In it he joyfully reported that "his waiting period was over" and that upon completion of a manuscript containing the "decoded message of the Seven Seals" he would come out. He considered the composition of this manuscript to be a privilege allowed him by God, the direct answer to his prayers which he had sought for the past seven weeks.

Although many questioned both the ability and intention of David Koresh to produce this manuscript, we received this news with great relief. We had been urging David for several weeks through radio broadcasts and cassette tapes to exit Mt. Carmel peacefully as he now proposed to do. We had based our case to him on interpretations of the Book of Revelation which we felt he might find persuasive. This was only five days before the tragic fire on April 19th.

We now know that David Koresh did begin work on his manuscript and truly took it most seriously. A computer disk containing his dictated text was carried out of Mt. Carmel by Ruth Riddle, a survivor of the fire. Indeed, Ruth tells us that she and David worked for several hours on Sunday night, the last night of his life; him dictating and she typing out his thoughts. She reports that the Branch Davidians were calm and joyful that evening at the prospect of David completing his work and their impending exodus.

David's work will speak for itself to those who are interested in his exegesis and understanding of the mysterious Seven Seals of the Book of Revelation. Regardless of one's evaluation of the content, one point is clear--in a short time, under most trying circumstances, David Koresh had produced a rather substantial piece of work. He had completed the Preface, which is a poem, the Introduction to the work as a whole, and Chapter One, which covered the First Seal. Judging from this work we can estimate that the finished product would have run about 50-75 pages and might have taken him another two or three weeks.

David Koresh, in that last letter, asked that the completed manuscript be given to his lawyer, Dick DeGuerin, then passed on first to us. He had apparently come to trust our knowledge and integrity in discussing with him his interpretations of Revelation. He then authorized our release of copies to scholars, religious leaders, and the general public. Although David died a few days later, and was thus prevented from finishing this work, we still thought it best to release this portion which he did complete, following his instructions. Actually, his exposition of the First Seal was perhaps the most vital in understanding his sense of his own mission, the reasons for the Waco siege, and what ultimately transpired.

The text is produced here precisely as it came to us from the computer disks. In the interest of accuracy we have also carefully consulted Ruth Riddle, who typed it on the Sunday evening before the fire. For the sake of brevity she did not type all of David's verbal quotations of scripture -- planning to insert them later. We have put these citations in *italics*. On rare occasions, we have supplied punctuation and a missing word in [brackets].

David's last sentence is a suggestive one which urges readers and followers to be ready to "come out of our closet." He calls upon those of us on the outside to forsake our own personal dark closets and he summons the Branch Davidians to "come out" of Mt. Carmel and face the world as lovers of Christ. Chapter One concludes with two scriptural quotations which promise the reader that God will one day re-establish David's fallen community.

Dr. Phillip Arnold
Dr. James Tabor
Rosh Hashanah, 1993

PREFACE

EDEN TO EDEN

Search forth for the meaning here,
Hidden within these words:
'Tis a song that's sung of fallen tears,
Given way for two love birds.

Love birds yet not of feathered creed
Shot down for gambled play,
And caged a far distance betweenst themselves
For the hunter felt is best that way.

"She bird is mine," the hunter said,
"'Twas this bird I raised and faithfully fed.
'Twas he bird who released her from her cage,
Sought her womb in youthful age."

Love birds the name, these birds they call,
Two, plural, love bird, takes two.
'Twas not her womb of which he sought,
And certainly not her youth.

Love birds the name, these birds they call,
Two, plural, love bird, takes two.
It's just that he needed she,
To fly the skies of blue.

And now we see the hunter man,
Robbed without a prey,
The evil which he sought to do,
Caused the birds to pass away.

For loneliness and solitaire,
Is death to every soul.
For birds of God were meant to pair,
The two to complete the whole.

And now we see the final meaning
Of this rhyme and verse:
The pending judgment of the King
Who rules the universe.

For with Adam and his spirit Eve,
To share the kingdom fair;
But when they sinned they lost their crown
In exchange for shame to bear.

So Eve travailed and brought forth death,
And passed the crown to all;
For each to learn the lesson here,
The kingdom of the fall.

For virgins do not bring forth sons,
Until God does reverse,
The inner meaning of the law,
To remove man from the curse.

For in the Christ, we've seen a bride,
The water mixed with blood,
The wife with cloven tongues of fire,
Of whom the Christ has loved.

And now He's back to sing His song,
The life of every spring,
And love birds gather, each one with mate,
For the Marriage of the King.

INTRODUCTION

[All scriptural passages are from the Authorized King James Version Bible and are in *italics*.]

Then Pilate entered into the judgment hall again, and called Jesus, and said unto him, Art thou the King of the Jews? Jesus answered him, Sayest thou this thing of thyself, or did others tell it thee of me? Pilate answered him, Am I a Jew? Thine own nation and the chief priests have delivered thee unto me: What hast thou done? Jesus answered, My kingdom is not of this world: if my kingdom were of this world, then would my servants fight, that I should not be delivered to the Jews: but now is my kingdom not from hence. Pilate therefore said unto him, Art thou a king, then? Jesus answered, Thou sayest that I am a king. To this end was I born, and for this cause came I into the world, that I should bear witness unto the truth. Every one that is of the truth heareth my voice. Pilate saith unto him, What is truth? And when he had said this, he went out again unto the Jews, and saith unto them, I find in him no fault at all. (John 18:33-38)

Stange indeed for the judgment of man, for who knows within himself that his judgment be true?

Scripture tells us that Pilate was convicted of the truth in Christ, but failing to take heed thereto, he lost his soul, causing the blood of the innocent to be shed. How many of us since the dawning of time have committed such things? Who was this Jesus? Who was this Saviour that nearly a whole religious nation rejected?

Matthew told us. Mark, Luke, and John all recorded their side of the story of which remains unto this day, read and judged of all. Likewise, the Acts, the Book of Romans, Corinthians, Galatians, Ephesians, and such books open for our learning this most unique mystery of judgment and justice undone. But of all the records the most awe inspiring remains to be the most misunderstood, that being the Revelation of Jesus Christ written by the Apostle John to the churches of Asia and left on record that all who follow may ask the question:

"Who is this Christ and what remains to be the mystery of Him?"

In my work to unfold this mystery to you I will not use great techniques of scholarly display nor in-depth reasonings of philosophy; no sophisticated, congenial language shall be used, just simple talk and reason.

First of all, *"The Revelation of Jesus Christ, which God gave unto him, to shew unto his servants things which must shortly come to pass"* (Revelation 1:1) is to be seen just as that: a revelation of Jesus to reveal to men His wishes and His desires for those who make up His church. For the kingdom of God being that of heaven, and not of this world, is to be revealed unto this world by the means He has chosen -- *"the foolishness of preaching."* [see 1 Corinthians 1:21] John the Apostle while on the Isle of Patmos received the Lord's messenger and in obedience placed in written form all that he saw and all that he heard pertaining to the mysteries of Christ. And in good faith the Apostle stated, *"Blessed is he that readeth, and they that hear the words of this prophecy, and keep those things which are written therein: for the time is at hand."*
(Revelation 1:3)

Likewise John was commanded of the angel, *"Write the things which thou hast seen, and the things which are, and the things which shall be hereafter."* (Revelation 1:19) Simply, John's record contains the past, present, and future events that revolve around the Revelation of Jesus Christ. John in faithfulness sent his writings to the seven churches in Asia and the will of Christ for these churches is plainly revealed from chapter 2 to chapter 4 of Revelation. Therefore on record, all may read and see how Christ has dealt with His churches of old.

Our subject of interest will be taken up from chapter 4 through chapter 22, for these passages entail the events that are to be after John's time. For it is written:

After this I looked, and, behold, a door was opened in heaven: and the first voice which I heard was as it were of a trumpet talking with me; which said, Come up hither, and I will show thee things which must be hereafter. And immediately I was in the spirit: and, behold, a throne was set in heaven, and one sat on the throne. And he that sat was to look upon like a jasper and a sardine stone: and there was a rainbow round about the throne, in sight like unto an emerald. And round about the throne were four and twenty seats: and upon the seats I saw four and twenty elders sitting, clothed in white raiment; and they had on their heads crowns of gold. And out of the throne proceeded lightnings and thunderings and voices: and there were seven lamps of fire burning before the throne, which are the seven Spirits of God. And before the throne there was a sea of glass like unto crystal: and in the midst of the throne, and round about the throne, were four beasts full of eyes before and behind. And the first beast was like a lion, and the second beast like a calf, and the third beast had a face as a man, and the fourth beast was like a flying eagle. And the four beasts had each of them six wings about him; and they were full of eyes within: and they rest not day and night, saying, Holy, holy, holy, Lord God Almighty, which was, and is, and is to come. And when those beasts give glory and honour and thanks to him that sat on the throne, who liveth for ever and ever, the four and twenty elders fall down before him that sat on the throne, and worship him that liveth for ever and ever, and cast their crowns before the throne, saying, Thou art worthy, O Lord, to receive glory and honour and power: for thou hast created all things, and for thy pleasure they are and were created. **(Revelation 4: entire chapter)**

John states that that *"which must be hereafter"* -- sometime after his day -- there will be a God who sits on His throne. There will be a jury of twenty-four elders. God will be declared as *"worthy ... to receive glory and honour and power,"* because unto Him and for Him all things were created.

John continues to say:

And I saw in the right hand of him that sat on the throne a book written within and on the backside, sealed with seven seals. And I saw a strong angel proclaiming with a loud voice, Who is worthy to open the book, and to loose the seals thereof? And no man in heaven, nor in earth, neither under the earth, was able to open the book, neither to look thereon. And I wept much, because no man was found worthy to open and to read the book, neither to look thereon. And one of the elders saith unto me, Weep not: behold, the Lion of the tribe of Judah, the Root of David, hath prevailed to open the book, and to loose the seven seals thereof. And I beheld and, lo, in the midst of the throne and of the four beasts, and in the midst of the elders, stood a Lamb as it had been slain, having seven horns and seven eyes, which are the seven Spirits of God sent forth into all the earth.

And he came and took the book out of the right hand of him that sat upon the throne. And when he had taken the book, the four beasts and four and twenty elders fell down before the Lamb, having every one of them harps, and golden vials full of odours, which are the prayers of saints. And they sung a new song, saying, Thou art worthy to take the book, and to open the seals thereof: for thou wast slain, and hast redeemed us to God by thy blood out of every kindred, and tongue, and people, and nation; and hast made us unto our God kings and priests: and we shall reign on the earth. And I beheld, and I heard the voice of many angels round about the throne and the beasts and the elders: and the number of them was ten thousand times ten thousand, and thousands of thousands; saying with a loud voice, Worthy is the Lamb that was slain to receive power, and riches, and wisdom, and strength, and honour, and glory, and blessing. And every creature which is in heaven, and on the earth, and under the earth, and such as are in the sea, and all that are in them, heard I saying, Blessing, and honour, and glory, and power, be unto him that sitteth upon the throne, and unto the Lamb for ever and ever. And the four beasts said, Amen. And the four and twenty elders fell down and worshipped him that liveth for ever and ever. (Revelation 5: entire chapter)

Very clearly John tells of a judgment in which only one question is asked, *"Who is worthy"* to open or to reveal a book found in the right hand of God clearly sealed with seven seals. John states, *"no man in heaven, nor in earth, neither under the earth, was able to open the book, neither to look thereon."* Then John is pointed to the hope af all men: the Lamb that was slain. Here is a revelation of Christ as our High Priest in heaven. Here His work is revealed: the opening of the mysteries of God. These mysteries of which reveal Christ and His sufficiency to save all whose prayers are directed to God through Him. Likewise Paul the Apostle has stated:

So also Christ glorified not himself to be made an high priest; but he that said unto him, Thou art my Son, to day have I begotten thee. [See next page for references of this and following quotations of Scripture.]

For the law made nothing perfect, but the bringing in of a better hope did; by the which we draw nigh unto God . . . But this man, because he continueth ever, hath an unchangeable priesthood. Wherefore, he is able also to save them to the uttermost that come unto God by him, seeing he ever liveth to make intercession for them.

But now hath he obtained a more excellent ministry, by how much also he is the mediator of a better covenant, which was established upon better promises.

For Christ is not entered into the holy places made with hands, which are the figures of the true; but into heaven itself, now to appear in the presence of God for us:

But this man, after he had offered one sacrifice for sins for ever, sat down on the right hand of God; from henceforth expecting all his enemies be made his footstool. For by one offering he hath perfected for ever them that are sanctified.

For if we sin wilfully after we have received the knowledge of the truth, there remaineth no more sacrifice for sins,

Of how much sorer punishment, suppose ye, shall he be thought worthy, who hath trodden under foot the Son of God, and hath counted the blood of the covenant, wherewith he was sanctified, an unholy thing, and hath done despite unto the Spirit of grace?

For ye are not come unto the mount that might be touched, and that burned with fire, nor unto blackness, and darkness, and tempest, and the sound of a trumpet, and the voice of words; which voice they that heard intreated that the word should not be spoken to them any more: (For they could not endure that which was commanded, and if so much as a beast touch the mountain, it shall be stoned, or thrust through with a dart: And so terrible was the sight, that Moses said, I exceedingly fear and quake:) But ye are come unto mount Sion, and unto the city of the living God, the heavenly Jerusalem, and to an innumerable company of angels, to the general assembly and church of the firstborn, which are written in heaven, and to God the Judge of all, and to the spirits of just men made perfect, And to Jesus the mediator of the new covenant, and to the blood of sprinkling, that speaketh better things than that of Abel. See that ye refuse not him that speaketh. For if they escaped not who refused him that spoke on earth, much more shall not we escape, if we turn away from him that speaketh from heaven:

(Hebrews 5:5; 7:19, 24-25; 8:6; 9:24; 10:12-14, 26, 29; 12:18-25)

Clearly then, John is showing us of that very event of which Paul the Apostle so clearly writes. Christ is the mediator of the New Covenant and that New Covenant is contained in the seven seals. If we the church have been so long awaiting that which must be hereafter, why is it that so many of us in Christendom have not even heard of the seven seals?

Why is this Revelation of Jesus Christ which God gave to Him such a mystery? The Apostle Peter gives us a clue when he said:

Blessed be the God and Father of our Lord Jesus Christ, which according to his abundant mercy hath begotten us again unto a lively hope by the resurrection of Jesus Christ from the dead, to an inheritance incorruptible, and undefiled, and that fadeth not away, reserved in heaven for you, who are kept by the power of God through faith unto salvation ready to be revealed in the last time.

(1 Peter 1:3-5)

Truly Christ is our only Saviour, our only Mediator between man and God. Likewise, it is true the opening of the seven seals by Christ is as much or more so important for our salvation as any other former gospels. If this *"salvation"* is *"ready to be revealed in the last time,"* as Peter says, then we should hear another statement from the Apostle Peter:

Wherefore, gird up the loins of your mind, be sober, and hope to the end for the grace that is to be brought unto you at the revelation of Jesus Christ; (1 Peter 1:13)

So the question remains -- What are the seven seals? And the answer remains -- a *"Revelation of Jesus Christ, which God gave unto him, to show unto his servants things which must shortly come to pass."* (Revelation 1:1) If these things were to "shortly come to pass" then surely they must have already been fulfilled, and if so, does that mean we are "His servants" if we know these things not? Or could it be that the "things which must be hereafter" pertaining to God's throne, the judgment, the book, and the Lamb receiving that book are events directed primarily to the last

times or the last days? If that's the case are we in the last days? If so, then it must be time for God's servants to know these things.

So teach us to number our days, that we may apply our hearts unto wisdom. Return, O LORD, how long? and let it repent thee concerning thy servants. O satisfy us early with thy mercy; that we may rejoice and be glad all our days. Make us glad according to the days wherein thou hast afflicted us, and the years wherein we have seen evil. Let thy work appear unto thy servants, and thy glory unto their children. And let the beauty of the LORD our God be upon us: and establish thou the work of our hands upon us; yea, the work of our hands establish thou it. **(Psalm 90:12-17)**

He that dwelleth in the secret place of the most High shall abide under the shadow of the Almighty. I will say of the LORD, He is my refuge and my fortress: my God; in him will I trust. Surely he shall deliver thee from the snare of the fowler, and from the noisome pestilence. He shall cover thee with his feathers, and under his wings shalt thou trust: his truth shall be thy shield and buckler. **(Psalm 91:1-4)**

If the foundations be destroyed, what can the righteous do? The LORD is in his holy temple, the LORD'S throne is in heaven: his eyes behold, his eyelids try, the children of men. **(Psalm 11:3-4)**

The servant of God will find as we continue in our searching of the scriptures that every book of the Bible meets and ends in the book of Revelation. Gems of most sacred truth are to be uncovered, golden promises never before seen are to be brought to view, for when has grace ever been needed more than now in the time of which we live?

CHAPTER 1

THE FIRST SEAL

Although we, the servants of God, do not live in Asia, we are nonetheless to be beneficiaries of their counsels; and they likewise, not being alive today are no doubt to be a part of the grace which we are to receive.

Revelation 6:1-2: *And I saw when the Lamb opened one of the seals, and I heard, as it were the noise of thunder, one of the four beasts saying, Come and see. And I saw, and behold a white horse: and he that sat on him had a bow; and a crown was given unto him: and he went forth conquering, and to conquer.*

Here in our Heavenly Zion we see the Lamb loose the first seal. This preview of God's revelation of His Son is to be of our utmost interest, for not only will it more clearly reveal the nature of Christ, but it will likewise unfold more clearly the Divine nature of God who is the Author of this revelation.

Now let's turn to Psalm 45:

My heart is inditing a good matter: I speak of the things which I have made touching the king: my tongue is the pen of a ready writer. Thou art fairer than the children of men: grace is poured into thy lips: therefore God hath blessed thee for ever. Gird thy sword upon thy thigh, O most mighty, with thy glory and thy majesty. And in thy majesty ride prosperously because of truth and meekness and righteousness; and thy right hand shall teach thee terrible things. Thine arrows are sharp in the heart of the king's enemies; whereby the people fall under thee. Thy throne, O God, is for ever and ever: the sceptre of thy kingdom is a right sceptre. Thou lovest righteousness, and hatest wickedness: therefore God, thy God, hath anointed thee with the oil of gladness above thy fellows. All thy garments smell of myrrh, and aloes, and cassia, out of the ivory palaces, whereby they have made thee glad. Kings' daughters were among thy honourable women: upon thy right hand did stand the queen in gold of Ophir. Hearken, O daughter, and consider, and incline thine ear; forget also thine own people, and thy father's house; so shall the king greatly desire thy beauty: for he is thy Lord; and worship thou him. And the daughter of Tyre shall be there with a gift; even the rich among the people shall intreat thy favour. The king's daughter is all glorious within: her clothing is of wrought gold. She shall be brought unto the king in raiment of needlework: the virgins her companions that follow her shall be brought unto thee. With gladness and rejoicing shall they be brought: they shall enter into the king's palace. Instead of thy fathers shall be thy children, whom thou mayest make princes in all the earth. I will make thy name to be remembered in all generations: therefore shall the people praise thee for ever and ever.

Verse 1: "*My* (God's) *heart is inditing a good matter:* I (God) *speak of the things which I* (the Creator of all things) *have made touching the King* (Christ): *my* (God's) *tongue is the pen of a ready writer.*" Here we see God not only creates all things by His Word, but in His wisdom He has chosen some things to be written, that by the power of His word He may bring these things to pass in His own time. Here we see God by His written Word foretelling his determined purpose for His Son, Christ.

Verses 2-4: *"Thou art fairer than the children of men: grace is poured into thy lips: therefore God hath blessed thee for ever. Gird thy sword upon thy thigh, O most mighty, with thy glory and thy majesty. And in thy majesty ride prosperously because of truth and meekness and righteousness; and thy right hand shall teach thee terrible things."* Clearly in the Revelation Christ is fairer than the fairest. Those who receive the seals receive the grace found therein. Christ is capable of destroying his enemies for His majesty truly is great in heaven, for it is witnessed that all angels bow before him. What is it that Christ shall ride but the white horse because the book given to Him is the truth and He shall ride prosperously.

Verse 5: *"Thine arrows are sharp in the heart of the king's enemies; whereby the people fall under thee."* Here we see the meaning of the bow of which the first seal speaks. Let us pray that none of us refuse *"Him that speaks from heaven"* and the Spirit of Truth that is now speaking from heaven for it is likewise written:

Verse 6: *"Thy throne O God, is for ever and ever: the sceptre of thy kingdom is a right sceptre. Thou lovest righteousness, and hatest wickedness: therefore God* (Christ), *thy God* (Father), *hath anointed thee with the oil of gladness above thy fellows. All thy garments smell of myrrh, and aloes, and cassia, out of the ivory palaces, whereby they have made thee glad. Kings' daughters were among thy honourable women: upon thy right hand did stand the queen in gold of Ophir. Hearken, O daughter, and consider, and incline thine ear; forget also thine own people, and thy father's house; so shall the King* (Christ) *greatly desire thy beauty: for he is thy Lord; and worship thou him."*

How can any man deny that the first seal is a preview into the event spoken of by the 45th Psalm? How important is this insight? How important is it to God, or to Christ, or to the church? While on earth Christ spoke many parables regarding His Kingdom and His Bride. Let's hear one and see if we cannot more clearly understand the importance of these things.

Matthew 22:1-14: *And Jesus answered and spake unto them again by parables, and said, The kingdom of heaven is like unto a certain king, which made a marriage for his son, and sent forth his servants to call them that were bidden to the wedding: and they would not come. Again, he sent forth other servants, saying, Tell them which are bidden, Behold, I have prepared my dinner: my oxen and my fatlings are killed, and all things are ready: come unto the marriage. But they made light of it, and went their ways, one to his farm, another to his merchandise: and the remnant took his servants, and entreated them spitefully, and slew them. But when the king heard thereof, he was wroth: and he sent forth his armies, and destroyed those murderers, and burned up their city. Then saith he to his servants, The wedding is ready, but they which were bidden were not worthy. Go ye therefore into the highways, and as many as ye shall find, bid to the marriage. So those servants went out into the highways, and gathered together all as many as they found, both bad and good: and the wedding was furnished with guests. And when the king came in to see the guests, he saw there a man which had not on a wedding garment: and he saith unto him, Friend, how camest thou in hither not having a wedding garment? And he was speechless. Then said the king to the servants, Bind him hand and foot, and take him away, and cast him into outer darkness; there shall be weeping and gnashing of teeth. For many are called, but few are chosen.*

Notice that in this parable of Matthew, Christ clearly teaches that those with indifferent attitudes who would not come into the Marriage Supper were to be slain. Their disinterest offended the King who we know is God. So, likewise, today if we disregard the truth of the first seal we really disregard Christ, who opened it and in so doing we disregard God who gave it. This indifference most surely will place one's salvation in jeopardy.

Matthew 21:42: *Jesus saith unto them, Did ye never read in the scriptures, The stone which the builders rejected, the same is become the head of the corner: this is the Lord's doing, and it is marvellous in our eyes?*

In this passage we see Christ pointing his hearers to the Rock (His God). We know in Revelation 4 God is pictured as one who appears to be a jasper and sardine stone. This one is the same stone to which Christ referred. So again we are reminded that what the Father gives to Christ is a revelation of Jesus Christ that God gives to Him to show unto his servants.

Was it really David who wrote the Psalms or was it God who spoke through David? Was it really the prophets who wrote their books or was it God who spoke through the prophets? If it was God, we must conclude God claims the book as His and we should more earnestly take it as God's Word.

We find now in Revelation 19 a verification of the events we have just read.

Revelation 19:1-13: *And after these things I heard a great voice of much people in heaven, saying, Alleluia; Salvation, and glory, and honour, and power, unto the Lord our God: for true and righteous are his judgments: for he hath judged the great whore, which did corrupt the earth with her fornication, and hath avenged the blood of his servants at her hand. And again they said, Alleluia. And her smoke rose up for ever and ever. And the four and twenty elders and the four beasts fell down and worshipped God that sat on the throne, saying, Amen; Alleluia. And a voice came out of the throne, saying, Praise our God, all ye his servants, and ye that fear him, both small and great. And I heard as it were the voice of a great multitude, and as the voice of many waters, and as the voice of mighty thunderings, saying, Alleluia: for the Lord God omnipotent reigneth. Let us be glad and rejoice, and give honour to him: for the marriage of the Lamb is come, and his wife hath made herself ready. And to her was granted that she should be arrayed in fine linen, clean and white: for the fine linen is the righteousness of saints. And he saith unto me, Write, Blessed are they which are called unto the marriage supper of the Lamb. And he saith unto me, These are the true sayings of God. And I fell at his feet to worship him. And he said unto me, See thou do it not: I am thy fellowservant, and of thy brethren that have the testimony of Jesus: worship God: for the testimony of Jesus is the spirit of prophecy. And I saw heaven opened, and behold a white horse; and he that sat upon him was called Faithful and True, and in righteousness he doth judge and make war. His eyes were as a flame of fire, and on his head were many crowns; and he had a name written, that no man knew, but he himself. And he was clothed with a vesture dipped in blood: and his name is called The Word of God.*

Notice how in verse 9 it says: *Blessed are they which are called unto the marriage supper of the Lamb. And he saith unto me, These are the true sayings of God.* Being the true saying of God, the first seal of Revelation 6:1-2 must be true according to the saying of God in Psalm 45. And how can we be *"blessed"* if we know nothing about *"the marriage supper of the Lamb"* nor what it entails?

Isaiah 33:17: *Thine eyes shall see the king in his beauty: they shall behold the land that is very far off.*

Are we starting to see the King a little more clearly? And how about that heavenly land very far off?

Isaiah 55:3-4: *Incline your ear, and come unto me: hear, and your soul shall live; and I will make an everlasting covenant with you, even the sure mercies of David. Behold, I have given him for a witness to the people, a leader and commander to the people.*

Has not David truly witnessed on behalf of God, by God's own power, this beautiful marriage of which all are called to receive the knowledge of?

Isaiah 61:8-10: *For I the LORD love judgment, I hate robbery for burnt offering; and I will direct their work in truth, and I will make an everlasting covenant with them. And their seed shall be known among the Gentiles, and their offspring among the people: all that see them shall acknowledge them, that they are the seed which the LORD hath blessed. I will greatly rejoice in the LORD, my soul shall be joyful in my God; for he hath clothed me with the garments of salvation, he hath covered me with the robe of righteousness, as a bridegroom decketh himself with ornaments, and as a bride adorneth herself with her jewels.*

We should surely at this moment realize the importance of learning more thoroughly the meaning of Christ according to the seals lest we be found without *"the wedding garment"* of God's judgment, for if we receive this enlightenment, this *"grace"* which comes from heaven, we shall surely be partakers of *"the marriage of the Lamb"* for we are the guests who will *"Hearken . . . and consider."*

Jeremiah 23:5-8, 18-20: *Behold, the days come, saith the LORD, that I will raise unto David a righteous Branch, and a King shall reign and prosper, and shall execute judgment and justice in the earth. In his days Judah shall be saved, and Israel shall dwell safely: and this is his name whereby he shall be called, THE LORD OUR RIGHTEOUSNESS. Therefore, behold, the days come, saith the LORD, that they shall no more say, The LORD liveth, which brought up the children of Israel out of the land of Egypt; but, The LORD liveth, which brought up and which led the seed of the house of Israel out of the north country, and from all countries whither I had driven them; and they shall dwell in their own land . . . For who hath stood in the counsel of the LORD, and hath perceived and heard his word? who hath marked his word, and heard it? Behold, a whirlwind of the LORD is gone forth in fury, even a grievous whirlwind: it shall fall grievously upon the head of the wicked. The anger of the LORD shall not return, until he have executed, and till he have performed the thoughts of his heart: in the latter days ye shall consider it perfectly.*

This beautiful prophecy, the Desire of the Ages, entails of Christ the Lord our Righteousness and also warns us of the latter days should we be found not standing in the counsel of the Lord.

If we, the church of God, stand in the counsel of Christ, especially in the light of the seven seals, shall we not be a part of that beautiful bride spoken of in Jeremiah 33?

Jeremiah 33:14-16: *Behold, the days come, saith the LORD, that I will perform that good thing which I have promised unto the house of Israel and to the house of Judah. In those days, and at that time, will I cause the Branch of righteousness to grow up unto David; and he shall execute judgment and righteousness in the land. In those days shall Judah be saved, and Jerusalem shall dwell safely: and this is the name wherewith she shall be called, The LORD our righteousness.*

She, the city, she, the saints, those who are clothed with the righteousness of Christ and His Word, for it is also promised in verse 17, *"David shall never want a man to sit upon the throne of the house of Israel"* for Christ remains a King *"for ever."* [see Psalm 45:6]

Ezekiel 37:24-25: *And David my servant shall be king over them; and they all shall have one sheperd: they shall also walk in my judgments, and observe my statutes, and do them. And they shall dwell in the land that I have given unto Jacob my servant, wherein your fathers have dwelt; and they shall dwell therein, even they, and their children, and their children's children for ever: and my servant David shall be their prince for ever.*

Daniel 12:1: *And at that time shall Michael stand up, the great prince which standeth for the children of thy people: and there shall be a time of trouble, such as never was since there was a nation even to that same time: and at that time thy people shall be delivered, every one that shall be found written in the book.*

If we are to be *"found written in the book,"* surely we should be found in the first seal, for where Christ is revealed shall not we also be revealed as one who *"hearkens and considers,"* for is not He *"our Lord"* and shall not we *"worship"* him *"in spirit and in truth"*? [see John 4:24]

In Hosea 2:14 we read: *Therefore, behold, I will allure her, and bring her into the wilderness, and speak comfortably unto her.* The Christian Church being scattered from Jerusalem went throughout all nations. Being amongst the Gentiles, the gospel was to impart unto the Gentiles the riches of God's mercy.

Verse 15: *And I will give her her vineyards from thence, and the valley of Achor for a door of hope: and she shall sing there, as in the days of her youth, and as in the day when she came up out of the land of Egypt.* Here it is promised that once the unfaithful ones as Achan are taken from amongst God's people we will definitely have a deliverance as all the prophets agree.

Verse 16: *And it shall be at that day, saith the LORD, that thou shalt call me Ishi* ['my man' or 'my husband']; *and shalt call me no more Baali* ['my lord' or 'my master']. If we are to call God by such an endearing term, we are to know Him a little better and how better to know him than in the Revelation of Jesus Christ?

Verse 17: *For I will take away the names of Baalim out of her mouth, and they shall no more be remembered by their name.* All false teachers and false prophets are to be forgotten for there is one God, and one Lamb, and one seven-seal truth.

Verse 18: *And in that day will I make a covenant for them with the beasts of the field, and with the fowls of heaven, and with the creeping things of the ground: and I will break the bow and the sword and the battle out of the earth, and will make them to lie down safely.* Just as Isaiah 11 has promised, so Hosea also promises, peace for those who are called to the Marriage Supper of the Lamb.

Verses 19 and 20: *And I will betroth thee unto me forever; yea, I will betroth thee unto me in righteousness, and in judgment, and in lovingkindness, and in mercies. I will even betroth thee unto me in faithfulness: and thou shalt know the LORD.* So again, here we see the importance of this opportunity of learning these seven seals and the complete entailment of what that includes.

Verse 21: *And it shall come to pass in that day, I will hear, saith the LORD, I will hear the heavens, and they shall hear the earth;* Are we not a part of this event by faith? Is not heaven in total unity to the receiving of these seals from God? Is not God's word supreme in heaven? And it being the Word which reveals Christ, now is the time like never before to pray that we may be worthy to understand these things more clearly.

Verses 22 and 23: *And the earth shall hear the corn, and the wine, and the oil; and they shall hear Jezreel. And I will sow her unto me in the earth; and I will have mercy upon her that had not obtained mercy; and I will say to them which were not my people, Thou art my people; and they shall say, Thou art my God.* (We will not go at this point into the in-depth meaning of the book of Hosea in every particular, for our primary subject at this point is the first seal and the Marriage is that subject.)

This should inspire us to look into the meaning of Hosea 3:5: *Afterward shall the children of Israel return, and seek the LORD their God, and David their king; and shall fear the LORD and his goodness in the latter days.*

Joel 2:15-16: *Blow the trumpet in Zion, sanctify a fast, call a solemn assembly: gather the people, sanctify the congregation, assemble the elders, gather the children, and those that suck the breasts: let the bridegroom go forth of his chamber, and the bride out of her closet.* Yes, the bride is definitely to be revealed, for we know that Christ is in the Heavenly Sanctuary anticipating His Marriage of which God has spoken. Should we not eagerly ourselves be ready to accept this truth and come out of our closet and be revealed to the world as those who love Christ in truth and in righteousness?

Amos 9:11, 14-15: *In that day will I raise up the tabernacle of David that is fallen, and close up the breaches thereof; and I will raise up his ruins, and I will build it as in the days of old: . . . And I will bring again the captivity of my people of Israel, and they shall build the waste cities, and inhabit them; and they shall plant vineyards, and drink the wine thereof; they shall also make gardens, and eat the fruit of them. And I will plant them upon their land, and they shall no more be pulled up out of their land which I have given them, saith the LORD thy God.*

Obadiah 21: *And saviours shall come up on mount Zion to judge the mount of Esau; and the kingdom shall be the LORD'S.*

COMMENTS AND CLARIFICATIONS

Drs. James D. Tabor and J. Phillip Arnold

David Koresh asked that his completed manuscript be given to us through his lawyer, Dick DeGuerin. Evidently he expected that we would read it with sensitivity and offer some reaction and evaluation based on our academic study of Biblical texts and our knowledge of the history of the interpretation of the Book of Revelation. The following preliminary comments will help the reader who is not technically trained in these esoteric texts to follow David's rather involved thinking and interpretation. Whatever one thinks of the Branch Davidians and their Biblical views, one can at least endeavor to understand their systematic interpretation of Scripture which they obviously found so compelling.

The key to understanding David Koresh and his perception of his identity and mission clearly centers on one question taken from the book of Revelation--"Who is worthy to open the scroll and to loose its seals?" (Revelation 5:2). The text identifies a figure known as the Lamb, or "Root [Branch] of David" who alone is able to open this mysterious book sealed with Seven Seals (5:5). Traditional Christianity has, of course, always understood this one to be none other than Jesus Christ of Nazareth. Hence the endless confusion as to whether or not David Koresh actually claimed to be "Jesus," or even God himself, for that matter. This manuscript makes it clear that he claimed to be neither, despite all the confused and misleading reports about his self-understanding. However, he certainly *did* claim to be this Lamb who opens the sealed scroll, as well as the figure who rides the White Horse when the First Seal is opened, and appears at the end of the book, still mounted on the same White Horse, when the "marriage of the Lamb" takes place (Rev 6:1-2; 19:7-19).

Part of the confusion has to do with the use of the term "Christ." This Greek word is not a name, but a title. It means "an anointed one" or to use the original Hebrew word, a "messiah." All the ancient high priests and kings of Israel were "anointed," and in that sense can be called "christ" or "messiah." This is standard Biblical usage. However, the Prophets began to focus on a specific and ideal Christ or Messiah who is to come. This one was to be a "Branch of David," that is, a descendant of King David, and would rule as a King in Jerusalem, bringing peace to Israel and all nations (Isaiah 11:1; Jeremiah 23:5). This Christ, like David of old, is also called the "Son of God" (Psalm 2:6; 2 Samuel 7:14). David Koresh clearly believed that Jesus of Nazareth was this Christ. However, he also maintained that the prophets foretold of another "Christ," a Branch of David, who would appear at the end of time and open the Seven Seals.

Psalm 45 is the key to the First Seal, according to David. Here the King is anointed, that is made "Christ," and rides his horse triumphantly (verses 1-7). This is parallel to Revelation 6:1-2 and 19:7-19--so this figure is none other than the Lamb. After conquering his enemies, the marriage feast takes place. This Lamb marries virgin "daughters" and has many children who are destined to rule with him over the earth (Psalm 45:10-17). Jesus of Nazareth, though anointed as Christ, never fulfilled this role 2000 years ago. Accordingly, David believed that Psalm 45, along with several other key Messianic texts, could not apply to this appearance of Jesus Christ of the first century. Jesus never married and had children, as this text requires. Psalm 40 also speaks of the same figure: "Then said I, Lo, I come; in the *scroll of the book* it is written of me, I delight to do thy will, O my God, yea thy law is within my heart" (verses 6-7). The text goes on to speak of this one as having "iniquities more than the hairs of mine head" (verse 12). This so-called *"sinful messiah"* is none the less the one written of in the scroll--which David connected, obviously, to the Seven Sealed Scroll of Revelation 6.

David believed that this same figure is mentioned in Isaiah 45:1 and called by name: "Thus says the LORD, to his *anointed* (christ), to Cyrus (Koresh in Hebrew), whose right hand I have held, to subdue nations before him ..." This Cyrus, or Koresh, is called Christ. His mission is to destroy Babylon. Historians have understood the reference to be to the ancient Persian King Cyrus, who literally destroyed ancient Babylon. But there is a deeper spiritual and prophetic meaning according to David, and for that matter, the book of Revelation. The whole religious-political system is called "mystery Babylon the Great." As the text says, "Babylon is fallen, is fallen," hinting at a *double* meaning and fulfillment (Rev 18:2). The last Babylon is defeated by the last Christ/King/Koresh, the "Branch of David."

In his manuscript David barely begins to get into the many texts of the Prophets who speak of this "Davidian" figure (Jeremiah 23:5-8; 19-20; 33:14-16; Ezekiel 37:24-25; Hosea 3:5). He makes the point repeatedly that this Christ comes in the *latter* times, and perceives that Jesus of Nazareth, who came 2000 years ago, never fulfilled these texts. The Lamb who opens the Seals comes right before the End, is humiliated and maligned, and like Jesus 2000 years ago, offers the world God's truth. In other words, David is regarded as the actual, final manifestation of the Lamb, who will fulfill these prophecies regarding the Messiah.

According to this perspective, the Waco standoff and "waiting period" was a test for all humanity. It did not have to end as it did. David believed that the world was being offered a chance to listen to this last Christ/Koresh, who could open the Seals, and thus show the way of repentance to our society. There was even an opportunity given for the actual decoding of the Seven Seals in written form, to be openly shared with all who wanted to hear. This was all cut short. The rejection and death of David, at age 33, around Passover time, became a strange repetition of the past. The Fifth Seal, which allowed for a time of repentance while the message went forth, ended with the "rest killed" as they believed Rev 6:11 predicted. The Branch Davidians now believe that the probation period is up, and the Sixth Seal of the Judgment of God is pending.

The manuscript indicates that those who respond to the message of repentance, who turn to God and begin following the Law of God, through accepting the Lamb / Koresh / Christ / King, will be invited to the "Marriage" feast. They are those "elect" ones who make up the Bride of the Lamb. He concludes this chapter with the thought that those who are truly part of the "Bride" are to come out of the "closet" and be revealed for who they are.

The manuscript also carefully maintains the distinction between the God the Father and His Lamb or Messiah. In that sense David Koresh never claimed to be God. However, like the Hebrew Prophets of old, and like Jesus of Nazareth, he did claim to speak the words of Yahweh God (the Father) directly, and in that sense could use, as they did, the first person mode of discourse.

The Poem, entitled "Eden to Eden," is quite fascinating. Like Paul, David implies that the "marriage of the Lamb" is a mystery which somehow rectifies what happened at Eden in the Fall (Ephesians 5:31-32). The physical sexual union ("the two shall become one flesh") has a deeper meaning, and involves the perfect bonding of "Adam and his spirit Eve" in the "new Man" to come. David taught the importance of the feminine side of the Divine and implies that Adam was created to express this dual image. However, through sin, Adam and his descendants were separated from the spiritual, feminine side, and remain in need of restoration. Through the revelation of Christ in the person of the Lamb, people are being reunited with their fragmented selves and gathered as lovers of God for the ultimate marriage union which will restore Eden.

DAVID'S PROMISE TO "COME OUT" AND THE EVIDENCE OF THE MANUSCRIPT

What evidence is there from the manuscript that David Koresh would have kept his pledge to "come out" of Mt. Carmel, as he stated in his letter to his attorney, Dick DeGuerin on April 14th? We know that the first chapter of this work was completed on Sunday evening, the night before the fire, and was typed onto a computer disk by Ruth Riddle. This disk survived the fire, carried out by Ruth Riddle in her jacket pocket.

The existence of the manuscript itself, as well as internal evidence within the text, confirm that David was keeping his promise to produce an interpretive document. Such evidence also supports the view that David actually intended to lead his group out peacefully. A literary analysis of the text clearly shows that David was not merely "pretending" to write on the seals, and that his pledge of April 14 was not a con or sham.

An analysis of this newly-released manuscript offers three reasons to conclude that David genuinely planned to compose a full written interpretation of the Seven Seals and that he intended, upon completion, to make this work available to the public.

First, the form and structure of the manuscript indicate that David's efforts were genuine, purposeful, and tangibly productive. After conceptualizing the project over that last weekend, David dictated to his typist on Sunday evening, April 18, in one long sitting of approximately four hours. The text consists of about twenty-five double-spaced pages of coherent and organized exegesis and commentary on biblical passages. Using both deductive and inductive logic, David presents his interpretation of biblical prophecy. Although his interpretation is unique in its specific application and reference, it is similar in method and style to other well known exegetes such as Isaac Newton, Joseph Smith, Ellen G. White, J.N. Darby, C. I. Schofield, or Hal Lindsey.

The structure of the manuscript is well planned and suggests that the author took pains to organize it in such a way that it would be well-received as a readable exposition. For example, the work begins with a preface consisting of a poem written by David. The poem is entitled EDEN TO EDEN and contains fifty-two lines divided into thirteen stanzas of four lines of metered and rhyming verses.

Further evidence of a careful hand at work appears in the section which follows the Poem. David entitles this section the "Introduction." It sets forth the hermeneutical principles and general themes which follow in the main body of the work. Following this Introduction the author begins "Chapter One," in which he turns his attention to the meaning of Seal One.

Chapter One is subdivided into major headings which consist of specific passages from the Bible. David comments on each of these biblical chapters and creatively associated them with the First Seal found in the Book of Revelation. In this way he combines insights from the Old Testament and the New Testament using traditional Rabbinic and Christian exegetical techniques. He closes with a clarion call for his readers to consider his presentation and decide for themselves if it is true. The Chapter ends with two biblical quotations, offering a sense of closure in regards to the First Seal and expectancy regarding Chapter Two on the Second Seal, which would have been dictated at the next sitting--probably on the very day of the fire.

The second indication within the manuscript that validates David's pledge to exit Mt. Carmel concerns the intended audience to whom it is written. Throughout the work David carefully directs his words to those on the outside of Mt. Carmel, assuming an audience who would not know the meaning of the Seven Seals. The writer's vocabulary, his style, and approach show that he expects that his words will be read by non-believers outside Mt. Carmel. It is evident that David attempts to persuade his hearers. The implied audience is non-Davidian. The writing and the delivery of the manuscript to the world would grant outsiders an opportunity to hear the message. Once the seals were delivered to the world, the need to remain in Mt. Carmel would be gone.

Finally, specific statements in the text support David's pledge to *"come out."* Ironically, the very last words we have from David in this manuscript read: "Should we not eagerly ourselves be ready to accept this truth and *come out* of our closet and be revealed to the world as those who love Christ in truth and in righteousness?" David not only expects some readers to accept his teaching, but he also prepares his followers inside Mt. Carmel to *"come out"* of the center. This is seen further in his reference to Joel 2:15,16, which is quoted immediately before his call to exit. This passage orders those in Zion (read: Mt. Carmel) to "gather the people ... assemble the elders ... gather the children" and infants and follow the bridegroom (read: David), "from his chamber and the bride out of her closet." The Davidians understood other passages from Isaiah to refer to their refuge at Mt. Carmel as a "chamber" where they could wait for God's intervention. This use of the term *"come out,"* drawn from Scripture, used in David's April 14th letter, and now appearing in the manuscript, clearly indicates what was on his mind.

Evidence from the manuscript indicates that David was in the process of fulfilling his pledge to "come out" and surrender to authorities, as he had come to believe God commanded. The waiting period inside Mt. Carmel had been necessary, he believed, because it caused the sinful world to focus its attention on the Biblical message of the seven seals. Had the world waited for David to finish writing the seals, it would have appeared to him worthy of mercy. He would hae considered his mission to bring his message to the world accomplished. David then would have been in position to leave Mt. Carmel as he pledged in his letter of April 14th.